Dana Jacobi

and the Editors of
Natural Health Magazine

Simon & Schuster
New York London Toronto Sydney Tokyo Singapore

The Natural Health

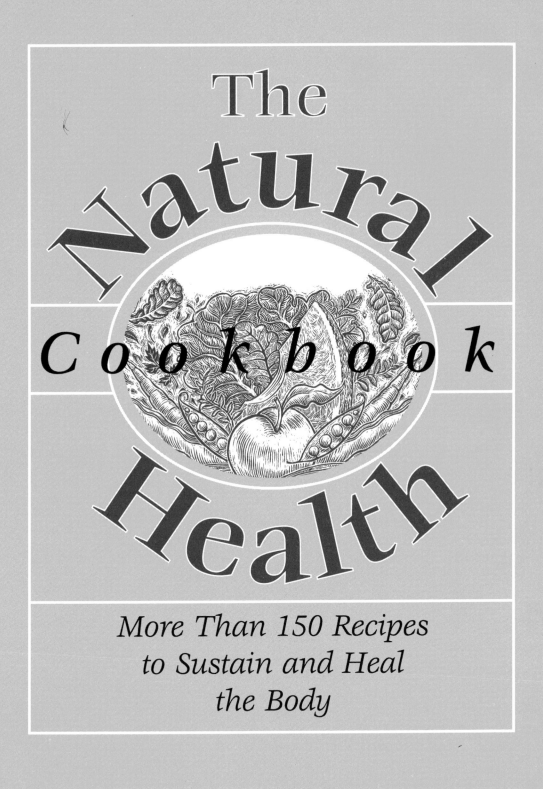

Cookbook

More Than 150 Recipes to Sustain and Heal the Body

SIMON & SCHUSTER
Rockefeller Center
1230 Avenue of the Americas
New York, NY 10020

Designed by Levavi & Levavi
Manufactured in the United States of America

3   5   7   9   10   8   6   4   2

Library of Congress Cataloging-in-Publication Data
Jacobi, Dana.
The natural health cookbook : more than 150 recipes to sustain and heal the body / Dana Jacobi and
the editors of Natural Health magazine.
p.   cm.
Includes bibliographical references and index.
1. Cookery (Natural foods)   2. Natural foods.   I. Natural health.
II. Title.
TX741.J29   1995   95-8
641.5′63—dc20   CIP
ISBN 0-684-80398-4

The recipes presented in this book are intended as educational tools to assist with improving food
selection and preparation habits. They are not diagnostic or prescriptive, and are not intended to be
used for therapeutic purposes without the advice of a qualified health professional.

Acknowledgements

This book was the work of dozens of people, as you can see from the contributors' list. It was initially assembled by Dan Seamens, former *Natural Health* senior editor, but is largely the brainchild of Dana Jacobi, who labored long and hard to select and edit the recipes and write the text. Thanks, too, to Sydny Miner, our wonderful editor at Simon & Schuster, and to these terrific cooks, chefs, and authors who have given us recipes over the years:

Karen Acuff
Cornelia Aihara
Timothy Aitken
Rick Albee
Johnna Albi
Colman Andrews
Akiko Aoyagi
Frank Arcuri
Indira Balkissoon
Karen Stein Bard
Rick Bayless
Jan Belleme
John Belleme
Kathleen Bellicchi
Barbara Benker
Jack Bishop
Terry Joyce Blonder
John Boyajy
Anne Burns
Ken Burns
Mary Carroll
Sandy Chianfori
Annemarie Colbin
Fran Costigan-Leeds
Patricia Curtan

Rachel Albert-Matesz
Lissa De Angelis
Machecha Diaz
Anne Westbrook
    Dominick
Pam Doyle
Edward Esko
Wendy Esko
Mary Estella
Leona Gadsby
Neil Garland
Lynn Gordon
Erik de Graaf
Marian de Graaf
Rose Grant
Rebecca Greenwood
Josephina Gundin
Crick Haltom
Lafcadio Hearn
Betsy Holliday
Barbara Jacobs
Leonard Jacobs
Eduardo Jimenez
Stephan Jimenez
Kirk Johnson

Charles Kendall
Martha Koetzsch
Ronald Kotzsch
Aveline Kushi
Martine Labro
Brenda Langton
Nam-ye Lee
Ron Lemire
Thom Leonard
Eleanor Lewallen
John Lewallen
Joan Livingston
Ted Louraine
Deborah Madison
Tess Mallos
Don Matesz
Chef Mark Miller
Meredith McCarty
Lauren McGuinn
Hamsa Newmark
Isobel O'Donnell
Lima Oshawa
Beverly Brough
    Painter
Bill Palmroth

Lynne Paterson
Jon Pell
Richard Pierce
Brother Ron Pickarski
Ramachandra Rao
Ann Rawley
Rachel Reid
Maritza Rojas
Daphne Rota
Linda Roszak
Genevieve Rowles
Derbhail Ryan
Satura Sato

Chris Schlesinger
Meg Seaker
Michael Shandler
Nina Shandler
William Shurtleff
Kathryn Silver
Celeste Skardis
Dongmee Smith
Scott Smith
Barbara Stacy
Eric Stapelman
Robbie Swinnerton
Gerry Thompson

Ana Troconis
Matt Venuti
Alice Waters
Marcea Weber
*The Whole World
    Cookbook*
    (EW Journal)
John Willoughby
Colby Wingate
Rebecca Wood
Jeff Woodward

Thanks to my mother, who continues to be ahead of her time in understanding what can be accomplished through diet and nutrition. Her open-minded approach to eating has provided the foundation from which I eat, work, and live. Deepest thanks also to Mark Bittman and everyone at *Natural Health* for inviting me to participate in creating this gratifying book.

—Dana Jacobi

Contents

Introduction

Every day, it seems, we hear more about how the foods we eat help us maintain or improve our health, or play a role in causing illness. For more than twenty years, *Natural Health* magazine has talked about how what you eat affects your well-being. We've covered the importance of eating a wide variety of foods, emphasizing whole grains and fresh fruits and vegetables. As Americans have consumed more and more refined and processed foods, like breakfast cereals loaded with sugar, frozen dinners full of fats, and snack chips packed with empty calories, we've explained the benefits of replacing them with more wholesome, homemade choices.

In recent years, scientists have come to join us, sharing information that documents the role your daily diet plays in helping to prevent or even reverse diseases. According to the 1988 U.S. Surgeon General's Report on Nutrition and Health, dietary choices are a factor in two thirds of all deaths in this country. The report stated unequivocally that the American diet is too high in fat and too low in fruits, vegetables, and whole grains. Learning to use these whole foods and the healing compounds they contain is a key to maintaining your health. But most Americans still haven't gotten the message. A National Cancer Institute study found that we consume a mere three and a half servings of fruits and vegetables each day—significantly lower than the five or more servings recommended. The truly shocking fact is that on many days, at least one in ten Americans does not eat any fruits or vegetables. And while variety is important to provide a wide range of nutrients, we tend to depend on a few common foods like citrus juices, bananas, and apples for fruits, and potatoes, tomatoes, and green salad for vegetables.

To help our readers add more variety to their daily diet, *Natural Health* has shown how to use a wide range of natural ingredients. We have also made choices about the best ways to support our readers in achieving an enjoyable, healthful diet. In particular, while we believe there is room on the table for most foods, we have focused on areas where good information is especially hard to find. This has led us to emphasizing vegetarian and vegan cooking—vegetarians do not eat meat, while vegans omit all foods from animal sources, including eggs and milk products—and using seafood, and to helping those with food sensitivities by offering dishes for people who avoid eating wheat.

Americans must change their eating habits. Before World War I, when Americans ate a diet close to what scientists and nutritionists now know is vital for good health, heart disease was unusual. Today, it causes 40 percent of all deaths in the United States, killing some 750,000 Americans each year. For 1989, the latest year for which information is available, the National Center for Health Statistics announced that six of the ten leading causes of death in the United States were chronic or degenerative conditions in which diet plays a prominent role. They are: heart disease, cancer, stroke, chronic lung diseases (bronchitis, emphysema, etc.), diabetes, and liver disease and cirrhosis. Along with these, other degenerative conditions have also become epidemic since the turn of the century, including arthritis, obesity, and immune disorders like Epstein-Barr syndrome.

Changing eating habits is tough, especially for generations brought up on highly processed convenience foods. To illustrate how much we need to alter what we eat, compare what people typically ate for dinner in the early years of this century with the menu an average family is likely to have tonight.

· Pickled cucumbers. Lamb stew with carrots, turnips, onions, and potatoes. Buttered boiled cabbage. And a dessert of apple brown betty with cream.
· Canned cream of tomato soup. Frozen fish sticks and french fries with ketchup and frozen broccoli topped with Cheez-Whiz. And dessert of Jell-O topped with Cool-Whip.

The first dinner provides two to three times the nutrients of the second at approximately the same cost, but with none of its scores of additives, although it contains plenty of saturated fats and cholesterol. The second is a menu in which many nutrients have been destroyed or removed and many additives have been introduced.

Those who have responded to the call for making positive dietary changes often find it hard to stick with these changes. After a few days, the thought of eating another bowl of oatmeal or brown rice palls. Figuring out how to balance the nutrition of meatless meals feels overwhelming. On the brighter side, when it comes to eating more fruits and vegetables, not everyone shares former President Bush's opinion of broccoli, or agrees with the child in the *New Yorker* cartoon who said, "I say it's spinach and I say the hell with it."

At *Natural Health,* we offer food that tastes good. We know lack of cooking skills is a reality that stops many Americans from preparing healthful meals for themselves and their family. This cookbook brings together information, assembled by the editors of the magazine, that will make it easier to enjoy meals that can make a difference in your life. It contains more than 200 of the most delicious, healthful recipes that we have shared with readers. These recipes use whole foods in ways that make eating a pleasure. They show you how to cook healing foods and incorporate them into your daily diet. The techniques you learn while preparing these dishes will also help you create family favorites in more healthful ways.

WHOLE FOODS

Advocating a diet of whole or natural foods raises the question of what these terms mean. To us, these are foods that are as close as possible to their natural state. They are either fresh or processed only minimally, with no artificial ingredients or preservatives added. Whole foods provide the maximum amount of nutrients in the way nature put them there. For example, whole grains are processed only to remove the indigestible outer hull; the bran and germ layers remain. Flour made from this whole grain also includes the nutrients found in the bran and germ. For wheat, this means you get all the B vitamins, vitamin E, and fiber nature put into the wheat berries. By contrast, white flour is made from wheat that has been stripped of the bran and germ; this flour is then enriched to replace vitamins lost when the bran and germ were removed. Enriching adds back only some of the B vitamins and iron, period. The vitamin E and most of the fiber simply are gone: you get bran only if it is specifically added back into the bread made from this flour.

ORGANIC FOODS

As part of a healthful whole-foods diet, we encourage you to use organically grown grains and produce. First, doing so allows you to enjoy foods that are grown using only botanical and biological pesticides and other chemicals not potentially harmful to the environment and to you. If you feel strongly about avoiding toxic chemicals in your food, seeking out food certified as organically grown may become increasingly important. More and more, the foods we eat are grown in and imported from other countries, some of which allow the use of agricultural chemicals banned in the United States. Since it is not always possible to know the origin of what you buy, chosing organic produce and other foods could be the surest way to know you are not getting something you do not want. Nutritionally, we recommend using organic fruits and vegetables, because worrying less about pesticide residues or wax may encourage you to eat their skins. In many instances, the skin and the area just below it is a rich repository for vitamins and minerals in fresh produce. This is true, for example, of carrots and potatoes. Generally, washing organic produce well should be sufficient to remove any undesirable residue on it. However, if you want to be absolutely certain of avoiding any chemical residues, then you can peel your fruits and vegetables. (Since not every single piece of produce is inspected during the certification process, and some chemical coatings are added at the store level, there are no absolute guarantees that certified organic foods never contain toxic chemical residues.) With organic produce, there is the possibility of easily recycling skins, peels, and trimmings to your stockpot.

Readers often ask how to be sure that foods labeled "organically grown" truly are. To protect consumers, many organic growers and food producers obtain "third-party certification." This involves having an independent group verify that the producer or grower has followed a set of production practices laid out in certification guidelines. About fifty organizations of farmers and citizens around the United States supply third-party certification. Organic Crops Improvement Association (OCIA) and California Certified Organic Farms (CCOF) are two organizations providing this service. The U.S. Department of Agriculture is currently working on a national set of certification standards that can be adopted by the entire organic foods industry.

When organically grown foods cost more than the same items at the supermarket, is the difference worth it? Food is the basic fuel on which our bodies run, so we believe in providing the best quality possible. In many cases, by shopping at farmers' markets and stores that carry locally grown produce along with milk, cheese, eggs, and poultry or meats from local producers, you may be pleasantly surprised. Many cities now have natural food supermarkets where you can get these and other items, including grains, cereals, nuts, and dried fruits, at good prices.

There is no perfect food, nor is there any one food that you can eat or diet you can follow to ensure good health. We feel the best diet is based predominantly on complex carbohydrates and includes the calories, protein, and fats appropriate to your requirements, based on your age and lifestyle. It also is a diet that provides most of its nutrients from whole foods, including fresh fruits and vegetables, grains, and legumes. Whether or not to eat animal products and seafood is your choice. If an occasional dessert includes butter, refined white sugar, and white flour; if you like bacon with your pancakes; if you go for a hamburger now and then, eating almost any food in moderation makes sense to us. What matters is helping you find ways to include in your daily diet foods that support your well-being and that you enjoy.

—Mark Bittman, editor in chief, *Natural Health* magazine

1. Soups

Here is a collection of distinctive recipes we have assembled—from light broths to rich, creamy soups and hearty minestrone—that show what can be done without the fat and cholesterol contributed by beef, poultry, or dairy products. Some call for ingredients found commonly in Asian cooking, such as miso, a flavorful soybean paste, and *kombu,* a sea vegetable used in Japan. Others show how you can make creamy, rich soups in unexpected ways. You'll find soups for every season and occasion.

There is no one foolproof way to make creamy soups and bisques without using dairy products. In some cases, the best choice is simply replacing cow's milk with plain soy beverage. In other recipes, the richness of a nut milk works better. Occasionally, miso creates a creaminess that, while different from that of cream or milk, is just perfect. Yet another way to obtain a lusciously creamy texture is by pureeing your soup. After making the recipes in this chapter, you'll have an idea of the most successful ways to rework your own favorite cream soup recipes to make them more healthful.

Since time is a critical factor, all our recipes call for either water or a stock particularly suited to the other ingredients in the recipe. When you do use water, it should be either cold running tap water or bottled water to avoid the possibility of a chemical taste.

Do you find a soup is better a day or two after it is made? That's because time allows the flavors to mellow, and reheating concentrates them further. This is why we like to make a big pot of soup and enjoy it for several meals. Another reason is that many soups freeze well. However, there are exceptions. Avoid freezing soups made with potatoes or lentils. The freezing process ruptures the cell walls of potatoes and lentils, and soups made with them will have a mushy texture when they are defrosted.

One final word of advice: add salt toward the end of the cooking process. You'll find this allows time for the flavors of all the ingredients in your soup to develop until you know how much salt is needed to balance the flavor. This is particularly important if you are using a prepared, salted broth. In this case, if you add salt too early on, you increase the risk of ending up with a soup that tastes overly salty.

Stock ingredients add nutrients as well as flavor. Homemade stock is almost required for good-tasting, healthful soups. By making your own stocks from scratch, you can eliminate a variety of unwanted ingredients found in commercially produced products, including excessive amounts of sodium and fat. Few do not carry risk from additives and preservatives. This tends to be true for commercially made vegetarian broth as well as for those made with chicken and beef. The few exceptions may be useful as time savers, but they do not taste nearly as good as homemade stocks and are expensive. If you use organic ingredients, you may also avoid possible chemical residues. This is true whether you are making a vegetarian stock or one that uses meat or poultry, where the animals have been treated with antibiotics and given feed treated with pesticides.

Use a full-bodied stock, and you can cut back on the salt and oil it takes to make a soup with depth of flavor. When you want a vegetarian stock, depending on the ingredients you put into the pot, you can produce some that rival the intensity of a classic French stock in just a couple of hours. Those made with mushrooms provide an intensity that can be particularly useful. If you eat fish, you may also want to experiment with Dashi (page 23), the smoky Japanese fish stock.

Basic Vegetable Stock

Stock serves as a foundation that ties together the flavors of all the other ingredients in a soup. This basic stock is suitable for making almost any kind of soup. We recommend you avoid using cruciferous vegetables such as cabbage, cauliflower, and broccoli because the strong flavors they add do not blend into most soups. Using them can also give a stock an unpleasant odor. This stock keeps well and can be stored in the freezer for up to 9 months.

3 ribs celery, with leaves, cut in 2-inch pieces
1 medium leek, with green top, cut in 2-inch pieces
1 medium zucchini or yellow summer squash, cut in 2-inch pieces
3 medium carrots, cut in 2-inch pieces
2 cloves garlic, unpeeled and crushed

Stems from 1 bunch parsley
3 medium onions, unpeeled and quartered
4 peppercorns
2 bay leaves
1/2 teaspoon salt
1/4 teaspoon thyme

In a 6-quart stockpot or other large pot, put all the ingredients. Add 12 cups cold water and bring pot to a boil over medium-high heat. Reduce heat and simmer gently. Skim off and discard scum that rises to the surface. When scum no longer collects on top of the pot, cover and continue cooking at least 35–40 minutes. The longer you cook this stock, the stronger its flavor. Strain stock through a very fine sieve or cheesecloth. Discard vegetables and bay leaves. Refrigerate or freeze stock.

Shiitake Mushroom Stock

The rich, meaty flavor of shiitake mushrooms makes this stock good for use in stews and brown sauces as well as in soups. Try using it, for example, in the Spiced Gingered Barley (page 45) and to make the filling for Kasha and Onion Piroshki (page 52). It is also a delicious base for miso soup. This simple stock can be made in a variety of ways, depending on whether you plan to use the shiitakes in a dish along with the stock or simply to give flavor to the stock.

6 *dried shiitake mushrooms*   4–6-inch-piece kombu (optional)
3 *cups warm water*

Place shiitakes in a bowl and cover with the water. Put a small dish or plate on the mushrooms to keep them submerged. Let soak for 2–3 hours and drain. The soaking water is the stock.

Cut off and discard mushroom stems, or save for making vegetable stock. Slice the caps thin and set them aside to use in soup or sauce.

If you are not using the mushrooms in a recipe together with this stock, soak shiitakes 15–20 minutes, then bring to a boil and simmer for 15 minutes. Remove shiitakes and reserve for another use.

If you are using *kombu,* add it to the shiitake stock when you begin to heat it. Remove *kombu* as soon as the stock boils, and discard or save to reuse for making a weaker stock. (The *kombu* will add a mineral taste to the liquid if it cooks for a long time.)

Use immediately or it can be stored for up to 24 hours or frozen.

Dashi
(Smoky Fish Stock)

This stock is the traditional base for miso soups. *Kombu,* a dried sea vegetable rich in calcium, gives this broth a delicate sweetness. Shaved flakes of dried bonito, a fish of the tuna family, add smoky flavor. Both ingredients can be found in Japanese food stores. Do not rinse the *kombu* before using it; any white, powdery coating adds to its flavor. Be sure to remove both the *kombu* and bonito flakes promptly or the dashi will be too strongly flavored.

6-inch-piece kombu   *¼ cup dried bonito flakes*

In a 2-quart pot, place *kombu* and 6 cups cold water. Bring to a boil and immediately remove the *kombu,* reserving it for another use.

Remove stock from heat, add bonito flakes, and let rest 2 minutes. Strain the stock, pressing flakes to extract all the liquid. Discard the flakes.

Serve immediately or it can be stored for up to 24 hours or frozen.

Shiitake and Watercress Soup

This is an elegant version of classic Japanese miso soup. Served along with brown rice, the protein in the miso and tofu make this soup fortifying enough to be the main dish of a light meal.

1 bunch watercress
4 cups Shiitake Mushroom Stock
   (page 22), or water
8 ounces firm tofu, cut into ½-inch cubes
¼ cup yellow or white miso

1 sheet nori, toasted and cut into 1-inch
   squares, for garnish
1 tablespoon chopped scallion, for
   garnish.

Wash watercress carefully by filling a large bowl with cold water, plunging watercress in, then draining. Repeat four or five times. Shake off excess water, and chop the watercress coarsely.

In a 2-quart pot, bring Shiitake Mushroom Stock or water to a boil. Add tofu, and simmer for a few minutes until the cubes expand. In a small bowl, mix thoroughly 1 cup of the stock with the miso. Return mixture to pot. Heat soup for 2 minutes more, without boiling. Remove from heat.

Gently stir in watercress and let the soup rest, covered, for a minute or so.

To serve, garnish each bowl with squares of *nori* and a few pieces of scallion. Serve soup quickly to retain the vivid green color of the watercress.

Lemon Escarole Soup

Escarole is the mildest-tasting member of the chicory family. It is a modest source of calcium. In this clear soup its bitter taste, which Italians believe aids digestion, is offset by the sweetness of carrots and daikon. Replacing the soy sauce with a ¼ cup of grated Parmesan cheese gives this soup a definitely Mediterranean flavor. Also try adding a cup of cooked rice just before serving if you want a more filling soup.

3 cups Basic Vegetable Stock (page 21), or water
1 small carrot, cut in julienne, at least 12 (1-inch) batons
¼ daikon radish, cut in julienne, at least 12 (1-inch) batons

3-inch piece kombu
8 escarole leaves, cut in 1-inch pieces, about 1 cup
1–1½ tablespoons fresh lemon juice, or to taste
3 tablespoons natural soy sauce

In a 2-quart pot, bring the stock or water, carrot, daikon, and *kombu* to a boil. Remove *kombu* and reserve for another use or discard. Continue cooking soup until vegetables are barely tender, about 3 minutes. Add escarole, and cook until tender, about 3 minutes more. Stir in the lemon juice and soy sauce.

If you multiply this recipe, steam or blanch carrots and daikon separately and add to individual servings of soup, so you don't have to fish them from the soup pot.

For a more festive presentation, slice carrots and daikon on diagonal and cut out with small hors d'oeuvre cutters.

Roasted Corn and Chili Chowder

SERVES 6

When corn is in season, this soup is a memorable way to enjoy it. Usually, chowders are made with cream or milk. Here, corn that has been pureed to release its sweet milk takes their place. Roasting gives the corn richer flavor. Chili peppers add vitamin C as well as heat to this soup. Whether you use fresh or dried chilies, be sure to use rubber gloves to protect your hands while cleaning them.

10 ears sweet corn in their husks
 5 cups Basic Vegetable Stock (page 21), or water
 4 dried Anaheim, chipotle, pasilla, or jalapeño chilies, soaked briefly to soften, deveined, seeded, and julienned

1½ teaspoons sea salt, or to taste
 1 tablespoon chopped cilantro, for garnish

Preheat oven to 400 degrees. Place ears of corn on a cookie sheet, and bake for about 45 minutes, or until the outsides of the husks are dried and brown. Allow to cool for 5–10 minutes. Shuck the corn, and cut the kernels from the cobs.

Puree 3 cups of corn with 3 cups stock in a blender or food processor. Place the puree, remaining stock, chilies, and salt in a soup pot, bring to a boil, and simmer, uncovered, for 10 minutes. Add the reserved corn kernels. Serve in bowls, garnished with the chopped cilantro.

Minestrone Americano

In Italy, beans and pasta make minestrone a meal in a bowl. Here, corn takes the place of pasta, supplying the nutrients of a grain and complementing those in the beans. When summer vegetables are at their height, make up a big pot of this soup, perfumed with fresh herbs. If you like, add a touch of Italy by serving it topped with freshly grated Parmesan cheese.

1 tablespoon extra virgin olive oil
1 cup thinly sliced onion (about 1 medium onion)
1 tablespoon minced garlic
2 tablespoons chopped fresh basil, or 3/4 tablespoon dried
1 teaspoon chopped fresh oregano, or 1/3 teaspoon dried
2 tablespoons chopped fresh parsley, or 3/4 tablespoon dried
5–6 large tomatoes, peeled, seeded, and chopped
1 cup peeled and diced potato (about 1 medium potato)

3/4 cup fresh or frozen corn kernels (1 medium ear)
1/2 cup diced zucchini (about 1 small zucchini)
4 ounces green beans (1-inch pieces), about 1/2 cup
1/2 cup cooked kidney beans
4 cups Basic Vegetable Stock (page 21), or water
1 teaspoon sea salt
1/4 teaspoon black pepper

In a large soup pot, heat oil over medium heat. Add onion and sauté for 1 minute. Add garlic and herbs and sauté for another minute. Add the rest of the vegetables, beans, and stock or water. Turn heat to high and bring to a boil.

Reduce heat and simmer for 1 hour. Add the salt and pepper, and serve. If you are using fresh herbs, you may also add more, to taste, just before serving.

MINESTRONE AMERICANO   27

Japanese Fish Soup

Light and elegant as a Japanese brush painting, this soup also is filled with assertive flavors. A brief cooking time helps preserve the vitamins in the cabbage and spinach. Serve this soup before a stir-fry or a hearty bowl of Spicy Soba Noodle Salad (page 65).

6 cups Shiitake Mushroom Stock (page 22)

1/2 teaspoon sea salt

2 cups thinly sliced carrots (sliced on the diagonal)

3/4 pound white fish fillets, cut into 1-inch pieces

2 cups shredded Chinese cabbage

2 cups loosely packed shredded spinach (cleaned and stems removed)

1/4 pound firm tofu, cut in 1/2-inch cubes

2 tablespoons natural soy sauce

1/8 teaspoon white pepper

1 teaspoon fresh Ginger Juice (page 241)

Chopped scallions, for garnish

In a large saucepan, bring the stock to a gentle boil. Add the salt and carrots; simmer 5 minutes. Add the fish and Chinese cabbage and simmer 2 minutes. Add spinach and simmer 5 minutes. Add tofu, soy sauce, and pepper; simmer 1 minute longer. Remove from heat and stir in the ginger juice. Ladle into bowls, top with the chopped scallions, and serve immediately.

Tangy Borscht

Fill your pot with layers of earthy fresh beets and their greens, plus cabbage and potatoes. Half an hour later, ladle out this robust soup. Beets are high in folic acid, which works with vitamin B_{12} to produce red blood cells. Topped with Tofu Sour Cream, chives or scallions, and an extra dusting of chopped fresh dill, this soup is a meal on its own. A green salad and rye bread make nice accompaniments.

4-inch piece kombu
1 cup sliced onion, (about 1 medium onion)
1 cup peeled and diced potato (about 1 medium potato)
2 cups chopped cabbage
1 cup chopped beet greens
2 cups peeled and cubed beets (about 2 medium beets)
6 cups Basic Vegetable Stock (page 21), or water, or more as needed

1 teaspoon dried, or 1 tablespoon fresh dill weed
4 tablespoons natural soy sauce
2 tablespoons prepared mustard
Salt and pepper to taste
1 cup Tofu Sour Cream (page 163), for garnish
1 teaspoon chopped chives or scallions, for garnish
Chopped fresh dill, for garnish

Place *kombu* in a large soup pot. Layer the vegetables in the order given, finishing with the beets. Add enough stock, or water, just to cover the beets. Cover the pot, bring to a boil, and simmer for 15 minutes. (The stronger flavor you get from cooking the *kombu* a longer time enhances the taste of this soup.)

Add the dill, soy sauce, mustard, and additional stock, or water, to reach desired consistency. Cook for 15 minutes more. Remove *kombu* and discard. Adjust seasonings. Serve, garnished with Tofu Sour Cream, chives or scallions, and chopped fresh dill.

Sweet Potato Soup

Sweet potatoes were a dietary staple throughout the Caribbean before Columbus came along and confused them with yams, a tuber indigenous to Africa. To this day, the pale yellow root we call a yam is almost always a sweet potato. Happily, sweet potatoes are richer in vitamins A and C than yams are. They are also a great source of beta carotene. The combination of ground coriander and thyme gives this soup an intriguing flavor. Its velvety texture comes from the combination of pureed sweet potato and soy beverage or milk.

2 tablespoons extra virgin olive oil
2 cups diced sweet potatoes (about
  1 large potato)
1/4 cup minced shallots
1/2 cup chopped celery
1 cup chopped onion (about 1 medium
  onion)
1/2 cup thinly sliced carrots
1/4 cup chopped fresh parsley

4 cups Basic Vegetable Stock
  (page 21), or water
1 1/2 teaspoons coriander
1/2 teaspoon dried thyme
3/4 cup plain soy beverage, or milk
1/2 teaspoon sea salt
1/4 teaspoon black pepper
  Chopped cilantro, for garnish

In a Dutch oven or heavy soup pot, heat the oil and sauté the sweet potatoes, shallots, celery, onion, carrots, and parsley for about 5 minutes, or until slightly softened. Add the stock, coriander, and thyme and bring to a boil. Reduce heat and simmer, covered, for about 1 hour.

For a chunky soup, puree half the soup in a blender or food processor. Return to the pot and add the soy beverage or milk, and the salt and pepper to taste.

For a creamy soup, puree all the soup in a blender or food processor. Return to the pot and add soy beverage or milk and salt and pepper to taste. Serve, garnished with the chopped cilantro.

Mushroom Almond Bisque

Mushrooms are not often thought of as nutritious, but they contain a good deal of protein, B vitamins, and copper and other minerals. Here, their flavor is enriched by savory miso and the sweetness of almonds. The miso and almond provide creamy richness without adding the cholesterol found in milk. A dash of paprika on top of each serving gives color and a perfect accent of flavor.

1 tablespoon sesame oil
1 cup diced onion (about 1 medium onion)
2 cups sliced fresh mushrooms
1/2 clove garlic, minced
1/4 teaspoon sea salt

1 tablespoon fresh lemon juice
1 tablespoon barley miso
1 cup Almond Milk (page 241)
1 tablespoon minced parsley, for garnish
Paprika, for garnish

In a soup pot, heat oil over medium-high heat. Add the onions and garlic, cooking until the onions are transparent, 3–4 minutes. Add the mushrooms and cook until they give up their liquid, stirring occasionally, about 4 minutes. Continue cooking until mushrooms are soft, about 5 minutes more, stirring occasionally. Stir in the salt, lemon juice, and miso.

In a blender or food processor, puree the vegetable mixture and almond milk with 1 cup water. Return soup to pot and heat through. To serve, garnish each bowl with parsley and a dash of paprika.

Indian Spiced Red Lentil Soup

Dal, a thin stew of lentils, peas or beans, is always part of meals in India because these legumes are an excellent source of protein. Some of these well-spiced *dals* are so close to soup that they can easily serve as a first course; this *dal,* which in a departure from tradition includes vegetables, is a perfect example. You'll find the small red to salmon-colored lentils called *toovar dal* used in this recipe at Indian and natural food stores.

1 cup red or green lentils
2 tablespoons mustard oil, or any light oil
1 tablespoon black mustard seeds
1 tablespoon yellow mustard seeds
1 tablespoon minced garlic
1 tablespoon minced ginger

$^1/_2$ cup thinly sliced onion (about $^1/_2$ medium onion)
1 teaspoon sea salt
$^1/_2$ cup thinly sliced carrots
1 cup broccoli florets
1 teaspoon Garam Masala (page 240)

Spread the lentils on a baking sheet and pick over to remove any stones. Place them in a strainer, and rinse thoroughly. In a heavy soup pot, bring 5 cups of water to a boil. Add the lentils, stir, and reduce heat to medium. Cook, stirring and skimming off scum occasionally. Remove from heat when the lentils are very tender, about half an hour for red lentils, 45 minutes for green.

Meanwhile, in a heavy skillet over medium-low heat, heat the oil. Add the mustard seeds and sauté briefly, until they begin to pop. Add the garlic, ginger, onion, and salt, and sauté, stirring frequently, for 5 minutes, or until the onion is tender. Add the carrots and broccoli and sauté 10 minutes more.

Stir the vegetable-spice mixture and *garam masala* into the lentils and serve.

Chilled Onion Almond Vichyssoise

Vichyssoise should be served icy cold, and is a refreshing treat on a hot day. Traditionally, this soup is made with leeks and cream, but this version uses almonds in place of cream to create a rich, smooth texture. You can use leeks in place of the onions if you like.

2 large potatoes
1 tablespoon sesame oil
1 cup diced onion (about 1 medium onion)
1 teaspoon dried basil

1/4 cup blanched whole almonds
3 tablespoons white miso
1/8 teaspoon black pepper
2 tablespoons chopped parsley, for garnish

In a medium pot, boil the potatoes in a generous amount of water and drain, reserving 3 cups of their cooking water. When the potatoes are cool enough to handle, peel and cut each into 5–6 pieces. Set aside.

In a skillet, heat the oil and cook the onion until translucent, about 4 minutes; stir in the basil.

Place the potatoes, cooked onion mixture, almonds, miso, and pepper in a blender or food mill, and puree until smooth. If using a food mill, mix together all of the ingredients, except the parsley, before pureeing. Chill and serve garnished with the parsley.

Chilled Ginger Pear Soup

Cold fruit soups are a summertime tradition in Scandinavia and Eastern Europe. Most frequently, recipes call for cherries or plums: we also like this perfect marriage of tart-sweet pears with spicy ginger. Pears are a good source of dietary fiber. Serve this soup as a starter for brunch or enjoy it for dessert with Poppy Seed Cookies (page 217).

8 ripe pears (any kind), peeled, cored, and diced
¼ teaspoon sea salt

4 tablespoons rice syrup
1 teaspoon grated ginger
Mint leaves or strawberries, for garnish

In a 2-quart pot, heat the pears, salt, and 2 cups water to a simmer. Add rice syrup and ginger and simmer 3 minutes longer. Cool. Put through a food mill or purée in a blender.

Chill. Serve garnished with mint leaves or a strawberry half.

VARIATION: For a creamier version, add 1 cup Almond Milk (page 241) and 2 more tablespoons rice syrup when blending.

2. Grains

We all know we should eat more grains. Rich in complex carbohydrates and protein, they are important for good health. Grains also offer a wide range of tastes and textures. Their amazing versatility has made them the darling of trend-setting chefs, inspiring these creative cooks to make good eating, with and without meat, a more healthful adventure.

Grains and grain products—bread, cereal, and pasta—provide about 50 percent of the world's calories. Yet Americans typically fall short of the six to eleven daily servings of grain recommended by the U.S. Department of Agriculture in its Food Guide Pyramid.

Finding appealing ways to use whole grains has long been a *Natural Health* trademark. We love them because they taste good and add satisfaction to a meal. We encourage readers to use them because they are such a good source of important nutrients.

Complex carbohydrates, which are primarily starches, are our bodies' principal source of energy. When you eat whole grains, you also get a wealth of B vitamins, including thiamine, riboflavin, and niacin, along with significant amounts of vitamin E, iron, zinc, calcium, selenium, and magnesium, plus both soluble fiber, which lowers blood-cholesterol levels, and insoluble fiber, which helps protect against some kinds of cancer.

Unfortunately, when Americans do eat grains and grain products, they are usually refined. This refining process strips away most of the fiber, B vitamins, vitamin E, minerals, and unsaturated oils from grains. Government regulations require that most rice and wheat products, including breads and pastas, sold in the United States be enriched to add back thiamine, riboflavin, niacin, and iron, but this does not nearly replace all the nutrients lost by removing the bran and germ. Even if you eat the recommended number of servings of grains a day, without whole grains it's less likely you will meet the daily intake of 20 to 30 grams of fiber recommended by the National Cancer Institute, for example.

Along with complex carbohydrates, grains are also an excellent source of protein. In fact, they provide almost 50 percent of the world's protein intake. Although grain protein is incomplete—low in some essential amino acids, like lysine, which act as building blocks for protein in the body—it provides all the protein your body requires when it is combined with small amounts of other proteins from foods like legumes, meat, dairy products, or eggs that are high in the missing amino acids. But average Americans get only 16 to 20 percent of their protein from grains, relying instead on fatty meats and dairy products.

Other cultures consume a variety of whole grains as staple foods: buckwheat, millet, quinoa, couscous, and bulgur, as well as brown, white, and wild rices, and corn. Our recipes are inspired by grain dishes from around the world as well as regional American favorites like jambalaya and cornmeal mush.

Keep grains in a cool, dark place. This is particularly important for whole grains, those with the germ and bran layers intact, because they turn rancid more rapidly than degerminated grains. A good way to store all grains is in glass jars in the freezer.

WHEAT—The primary grain in the United States and Europe. There are three strains. *Hard,* or *winter wheat,* is high in protein and gluten. It is preferred for bread baking. *Soft,* or *spring wheat,* is lower in protein and gluten. It is the best choice for cakes and pastry making. *Durum wheat* is highest in protein and gluten. It is used to make semolina, from which pasta is made.

Bulgur is made from wheat kernels that have been steamed, dried, and crushed. *Couscous* is made from durum semolina. Natural food stores carry both regular and whole-wheat couscous. Both kinds cook quickly and are good for salads, hot cereals, and North African dishes.

RICE—There are more than 25,000 varieties of rice. It is the primary grain for more than half the world's population, particularly throughout Asia. In the United States, rice is cultivated in Texas, California, Louisiana, and Arkansas. Brown rice retains the bran and germ. White rices have these layers polished away. Enriched white rice is coated with a layer to replace vitamins and iron lost in this process. Do not rinse enriched rice; it will wash off this layer.

Rice is also categorized by the length of its grain. Long-grain rices, which include basmati and some other aromatic varieties, are the most fluffy when cooked. Medium-grain rices are more chewy and sticky. Short-grain varieties are the most sticky and chewy. They go well with stir-fry dishes.

Wild rice is actually an aquatic grass grown in Minnesota, northern Michigan, Canada, and California. Wild rice is graded by length. The longest grains indicate the finest quality; they are also the most expensive. Buy shorter-grained wild rice and you can enjoy the distinctive flavor of wild rice for less money.

CORN *(Maize)*—Actually considered a vegetable in its fresh form and a grain when dried. A grass native to the New World, it is the basic starch for Central and South America, where it is traditionally ground to make tortillas and tamales. In the United States, dried corn is made into hominy, grits, and meal. Italians make cornmeal mush called *polenta.* Blue corn, grown in the southwestern United States, is higher in lysine than yellow and white corn varieties. This makes it a more complete protein than other types of corn.

BARLEY—This easily digested grain has been planted in Asia since around 7000 B.C. Rich in pectin, a soluble fiber, it is now eaten primarily in the Near East and Eastern Europe. In America, it is used mainly for brewing. Hulled whole or Scotch barley, sold mostly in natural food stores, has only the outer hull removed. Pearled barley has been polished and steamed to remove yet another layer, called the aleurone, which is rich in nutrients. Pearled barley cooks more quickly and is found in supermarkets in coarse, medium, and fine sizes.

BUCKWHEAT (called *kasha* when toasted)—Another grain that is technically a fruit (it is related to rhubarb), buckwheat is especially high in protein. Buckwheat cooks quickly. To keep the kernels separate and fluffy, buckwheat is sometimes coated with raw egg before it is cooked.

MILLET—A small, golden grain cultivated since at least the Neolithic era, it is a mainstay for nearly a third of the world's population, especially in Africa and

Asia. In the United States, it is used mainly for birdseed. Millet is particularly high in protein, contains no gluten, and is easy to digest.

OATS—Natural food stores carry hulled whole oats (oat groats) and rolled oak flakes. More pressure is applied during rolling to make thinner, quick-cooking oat flakes. There is no nutritional difference between these two kinds of oatmeal. Irish oatmeal, also called *steel-cut oats,* is coarsely chopped whole groats.

QUINOA—A protein-rich ancient grain native to the Andes, it must be rinsed well to wash off an outer layer of saponin. This soapy substance is a natural protective coating that imparts a bitter taste if not removed before cooking.

Other ancient grains, particularly kamut and spelt—non-hybrid varieties of wheat—and amaranth, are also worth looking for when you visit your natural food store. Try cooking them as you would rice or millet.

COOKING GRAINS

Toasting improves the flavor and texture of many grains. We recommend it particularly for brown rice, barley, millet, and quinoa. Put the rinsed, well-drained grain in a heavy skillet over medium-high heat and cook, stirring constantly, until you smell a toasty aroma. The grain will color slightly, but take care not to let it burn. Transfer to a saucepan, add water, and cook as usual.

Grains can be cooked using stock in place of water. When you are serving a plain grain, this adds extra flavor. When a grain has finished cooking, we suggest letting it stand, covered, for about five minutes. Doing this produces a fluffier texture. Just before serving, use the tines of a fork to separate the individual kernels of grain.

Some people prefer making brown rice in a pressure cooker rather than boiling or steaming it. It is not a quicker method, but the rice does come out with a nicely chewy texture and a slightly sweeter taste.

If cooking grains intimidates you, start with the basic recipes. We think you'll eventually discover all these dishes are comfortable to make. When you want a change from meat and dairy, when you need a side dish for any meal, or when you plan a vegetarian menu, here are a range of possibilities, from hot dishes to cold salads.

Pressure-cooked Brown Rice

2 cups short- or medium-grain brown rice   ¼ teaspoon sea salt

Place rice, 2½ cups water, and salt in pressure cooker and bring up to high pressure. Reduce heat, place flame-tamer under pot, and cook 45–60 minutes. Be sure the pressure is high enough to create a gentle hiss throughout cooking.

Boiled Rice

Nutritionally, boiled rice is the same as pressure-cooked rice, but its texture is lighter and fluffier. Using a fork to fluff the cooked rice is important to avoid crushing it.

⅛ teaspoon sea salt

1 cup short-, medium-, or long-grain brown rice

Place 2 cups water and the salt in a heavy 1-quart pot and bring to a boil. Add the rice, stir, and bring to a boil again. Reduce heat, cover tightly, and simmer 30 minutes. Place a flame-tamer under the pot and cook 20–30 minutes longer or until done. Fluff with a fork into serving bowl.

PRESSURE-COOKED   BROWN   RICE   39

Radish Rice Salad with Walnut Pesto Dressing

Why limit yourself to using vitamin C–rich, cancer-fighting radishes as a garnish? In this light rice salad, their color and crunch add to an intriguing mix of flavors. Serve it warm with broiled fish or take it along on a picnic to serve at room temperature.

3 cups cooked rice, white or brown
1 cup chopped toasted walnuts
1 cup chopped fresh basil
1 tablespoon minced garlic
1/4 cup fresh lemon juice

1/4 cup extra virgin olive oil
1 teaspoon sea salt
1 tablespoon white wine vinegar
1/2 cup thinly sliced red radishes (cut in half and sliced into thin half-moons)

In a bowl, combine the rice and walnuts. Place the basil, garlic, lemon juice, oil, salt, and vinegar in a blender and process until well mixed. Mix into the rice and walnuts along with the radishes, reserving a few radish slices to arrange on top as a garnish.

This salad is good made with warm, freshly cooked rice as well as with leftover cooled rice.

Millet and Rice with Spicy Peanut Sauce

SERVES 6

Millet has the most complete protein of all the grains and is also high in minerals. In this dish, its delicate flavor contrasts perfectly with nutty brown rice. This satisfying pilaf can be served as an accompaniment to a stir-fry without the Spicy Peanut Sauce.

1 cup medium-grain brown rice
1 cup millet

1 teaspoon sea salt, or to taste
Spicy Peanut Sauce (recipe follows)

Combine the grains, wash, and drain them well. Toast them, stirring constantly, in a cast-iron skillet or heavy stainless-steel pan over medium-low heat until dry and fragrant, about 15 minutes. Add 3½ cups water and salt, and bring to a boil. Reduce heat and simmer, covered, for 50–60 minutes, until the rice is done. Fluff with a fork. Mix with the peanut sauce and serve immediately.

Spicy Peanut Sauce

MAKES 2½ CUPS

1 tablespoon dark sesame oil, or ½
tablespoon each dark and light
1 small onion, diced
1 tablespoon minced garlic
1½ teaspoons bottled hot pepper sauce
¼ cup natural soy sauce
1 teaspoon ground cumin

¼–1 teaspoon cayenne pepper, to taste
1 teaspoon Chinese five-spice powder
1 cup smooth peanut butter
3 tablespoons maple syrup
2 tablespoons fresh lemon juice
1 cup chopped chives, parsley, or
cilantro for garnish

Place a small skillet over medium heat and add the oil. Add the onion and garlic, and sauté until the onion is translucent, 3–5 minutes. Add the hot pepper sauce, soy sauce, cumin, cayenne, and five-spice powder, and cook 2 minutes, stirring. Remove from heat.

In a bowl combine the peanut butter, maple syrup, lemon juice, and 1 cup water. Add the onion-spice mixture and mix well. Add the chives, parsley, or cilantro.

This sauce is also good on pasta.

Aromatic Basmati Rice

Few rices have the flavor and aroma of Indian basmatis. Even simply boiled, with no embellishments, they are delicious. The imported white basmati sold in Asian and Indian markets is an indigenous variety grown in the foothills of the Himalayas and aged for at least six months, and up to several years. (Aging dries the rice and heightens flavor.) The brown basmati rice available at natural food stores is not a true Indian basmati; while it tastes similar, it lacks the full fragrance of the real thing. Although not as nutritious as the brown variety, white basmati is a welcome change of pace in an otherwise whole-grain diet.

2 cups white basmati rice

Wash rice to remove dust and starch. Place measured rice in a large bowl and fill it with cold water. Carefully pour off water, and repeat 4 or 5 times until water is clear. Place drained rice and 4 cups water in a 1-quart sauce-pan, and soak 30 minutes.

Place pan on the stove and bring to a boil over medium-high heat. Reduce heat to simmer, cover tightly, and cook 15 minutes, or until the surface of the rice is pocked with little holes and most of the water is absorbed. Turn heat to very low and steam 5–10 minutes longer, or until all water is absorbed. Fluff into serving bowl.

Brown Basmati Rice Salad

True brown Indian basmati rice is more aromatic than the so-called brown basmati varieties grown in this country. Look for the imported kind in Indian food stores. Tossed with sweet peppers, rich pistachio nuts, and a brightly flavored dressing, either variety of brown basmati rice works well in this fresh-tasting salad.

 2 cups cooked brown basmati rice
1/4 cup minced red onion
1/2 cup diced red bell pepper
1/2 cup unsalted pistachio nuts, coarsely chopped
1/2 cup chopped celery

1/4 cup balsamic vinegar, or fresh lemon juice
1/4 cup extra virgin olive oil
1 1/2 tablespoons natural soy sauce
 1 teaspoon dried oregano
12 leaves red lettuce, for garnish

In a large bowl, combine the rice, onion, pepper, nuts, and celery.

In a small bowl mix the vinegar, oil, soy sauce, and oregano. Toss the salad with the dressing and chill for an hour. This salad will keep for 2–3 days refrigerated. To serve, make a bed of the lettuce leaves and top with the salad.

Wild and Saffron Basmati Rice

Cook the wild and basmati rices separately and then blend them together to create this elegant dish. Its golden color and sophisticated combination of herbs and spices warmed with orange zest make it festive enough for special occasions. Serve it with grilled salmon or vegetable kebabs. Add a handful of raisins and sliced almonds to leftovers, and you'll have a delicious rice salad.

Wild Rice

½ cup wild rice
1 sprig fresh thyme, or ½ teaspoon dried
1 sprig fresh rosemary, or ½ teaspoon
 dried, ground

1 bay leaf
Pinch sea salt

Rinse the wild rice. Place in a 1-quart saucepan with the sprigs of thyme and rosemary, bay leaf, and salt. Add 2 cups water. Cover and bring to a boil. Lower heat and simmer gently 45 minutes or until the grains begin to pop open and most of the liquid has been absorbed. Discard the bay leaf and strain off any extra liquid.

Saffron Basmati Rice

1½ cups white basmati rice
1 teaspoon extra virgin olive oil
2¾ cups boiling water
 Pinch saffron

7–8 cardamom pods, or ¼ teaspoon
 ground cardamom
1 × 3-inch-strip orange zest
 Pinch white pepper
 Pinch sea salt

Check rice for any stones. Rinse the rice and place in a medium-size heavy saucepan. Drizzle the rice with olive oil and add the boiling water. Add saffron, cardamom, orange zest, pepper, and salt. Stir, cover, and bring to a boil. Lower heat and slowly simmer 15 minutes, until the liquid is absorbed.

Remove the cardamom pods and orange zest, and fluff with a fork.

To serve, in a bowl, combine the cooked, drained wild rice with the cooked saffron rice. Mix gently.

Spiced Gingered Barley

Prepared pilaf-style, barley cooks up with a fluffy texture and a flavor that is reminiscent of mushrooms. Mixing the barley into squash cooked with sesame seeds and ginger makes a rice dish packed with beta carotene, calcium, and fiber. Just add a fresh green salad and complete your menu with cookies and tea.

1 cup barley
1 teaspoon fennel seeds
$1/2$ teaspoon anise seeds
1 tablespoon plus 2 teaspoons extra virgin olive oil
  Sea salt to taste
$1/4$ cup currants
7 whole cloves, or $1/4$ teaspoon ground cloves

1 × 3-inch-strip orange zest
$2^{1}/4$ cups boiling water
2 tablespoons peeled and minced fresh ginger
2 cups grated butternut squash (in long shreds)
$1^{1}/2$ cups chopped celery
3 tablespoons sesame seeds, toasted

Preheat oven to 350 degrees. Check the barley for any tiny stones or grains that still have hulls. Wash and drain the barley, shaking off excess liquid. Place barley on baking tray and bake 10–15 minutes. Stir every 5 minutes so that the grain toasts evenly. When the barley has completely dried and has begun to turn light gold and fragrant, sprinkle the fennel and anise seeds over barley and toast for an additional 2 minutes.

Place the toasted barley seeds in a heavy 1-quart pot. Drizzle with 1 teaspoon of the olive oil. Add a pinch of sea salt, stir, and add the currants.

(continued on next page)

Spiced Gingered Barley (*cont.*)

If using ground cloves, add at this point. If using whole cloves, press them into orange zest and add the orange zest to the barley. Add boiling water and stir. Bring contents of pot to a boil, then lower heat, cover pot, and simmer slowly for 45 minutes or until the liquid has been absorbed. Remove and discard orange zest.

Meanwhile, in a heavy skillet, heat the remaining oil, add the minced ginger, and sauté 1–2 minutes. Add the grated squash and a pinch of sea salt, stirring frequently for several minutes as the squash cooks. Stir in the celery. Cover the skillet to allow the vegetables to steam slightly. Once the squash and celery are tender add some of the sesame seeds and stir. Finally mix in the cooked barley. Adjust seasonings and serve garnished with additional sesame seeds.

Basic Quinoa

SERVES 3–4

Nutritionally, quinoa is truly a supergrain. It provides more iron than other grains and contains high levels of potassium and riboflavin. Quinoa is also a good source of vitamin B$_6$, manganese, zinc, copper, and folic acid; and, unlike other grains, its protein is not low in the amino acid lysine.

1 cup quinoa   *Pinch sea salt*

Rinse the quinoa several times and strain. Place 2 cups water and salt in a 1-quart saucepan and bring to a rapid boil. Add the quinoa, reduce heat, cover, and simmer until all the water is absorbed, 15–20 minutes.

Quinoa Timbales with Pine Nuts

A timbale is a deep-sided mold. Grain, often mixed with vegetables or meat and packed into such a mold, forms a decorative mounded shape, also called a "timbale," when unmolded. The blend of ingredients in this recipe creates an appealing Mediterranean flavor. This protein-rich dish is good served with steamed greens such as spinach or kale.

1 teaspoon unsalted butter
2 cups Basic Vegetable Stock (page 21)
1 cup quinoa, rinsed and drained
1/2 cup currants
1/2 cup thinly sliced scallions
1/2 cup pine nuts

1 tablespoon minced fresh parsley
3 tablespoons fresh lemon juice
1/4 teaspoon ground cardamom
3 tablespoons extra virgin olive oil
1/4 teaspoon sea salt
1/4 teaspoon black pepper

In a saucepan combine the butter and stock. Bring to a boil and stir in the quinoa and currants. Cover, reduce heat, and simmer 15–20 minutes or until the liquid is absorbed. Remove from heat and allow to stand 8–10 minutes, covered. Fluff with a fork. Stir in the scallions, pine nuts, and parsley.

In a small bowl whisk together the lemon juice, cardamom, oil, salt, and pepper. Toss the warm quinoa mixture with the dressing. Pack the mixture firmly into five lightly oiled 3/4-cup timbales (or small teacups) and unmold the timbales onto plates.

Quinoa Jambalaya

Here is a protein-packed but meatless version of the popular Creole dish. Delicately spiced, it's just hot enough to stimulate your taste buds. Tomatoes and green bell peppers add vitamin C, along with flavor. Serve with a side of collard greens and Pecan Sweet Potato Pie (page 231) for dessert.

1 tablespoon hot pepper sesame oil
1 tablespoon whole-wheat flour
1 cup diced onions
1 clove garlic, minced
2¼ cups diced tomatoes
1 bay leaf
½ tablespoon dried thyme
1 teaspoon hot pepper sauce

¾ teaspoon sea salt
¾ cup Basic Vegetable Stock (page 21)
1 cup quinoa, washed and drained
1 cup diced green bell pepper
½ cup chopped parsley
1 cup chopped celery
2 scallions, thinly sliced
¼ teaspoon black pepper, or to taste

Heat the oil in a heavy saucepan. Add the flour and stir until it releases a fragrant aroma, about 3 minutes. Add the onion, garlic, tomatoes, bay leaf, thyme, hot pepper sauce, and salt. Mix and simmer, covered, for 10 minutes. Remove and measure. Add enough stock so that mixture equals 2¾ cups. Return to saucepan, and bring to a boil. Add the quinoa, green pepper, parsley, celery, and scallions. Cover and cook over medium heat for 20 minutes. Turn heat off and let sit, covered, for 10 minutes. Remove the bay leaf, add the black pepper, mix well, and serve.

Double Cornmeal Mush

Whole corn kernels add texture and flavor to this humble all-American dish. Use whole cornmeal from a natural food store rather than the degerminated kind sold in your supermarket. No germ means a longer shelf life; it also means no flavor and little nutritive value. Serve this along with Sweet Pepper Pinto Bean Chili (page 120). Also try it for breakfast crisped in butter and topped with maple syrup.

1 teaspoon sea salt
1½ cups yellow cornmeal

1 cup cooked fresh or frozen corn kernels (1 large ear)

In medium saucepan, bring 3½ cups of water to a boil. Add the salt and reduce to a simmer. In a bowl, stir together the cornmeal and 1 cup cold water until smooth. Pour the cornmeal slowly into the simmering water, stirring constantly to prevent lumps. Simmer, uncovered, for 20 minutes, stirring frequently. Keep the heat very low to prevent scorching. Stir in the corn kernels, then simmer for another 15 minutes, continuing to stir frequently. The cooked cornmeal should be thick enough to hold together.

Pour the cornmeal onto an ungreased baking sheet or cookie tray and spread to ½-inch thickness. Allow to cool. This cornmeal mush can be stored for up to 2 days in the refrigerator.

Italian Baked Polenta Squares

SERVES 2

We recommend using the imported, coarsely ground cornmeal called polenta sold at Italian food stores for this dish. Constantly stirring the polenta as it cooks gives it a creamy texture. Italians often serve polenta topped with a rich tomato sauce. Parmesan cheese is the most calcium-rich of all cheeses; to keep the fat content in this dish low, we add just a touch for flavor.

2 (3-inch) squares Double Cornmeal Mush (page 49)
$1/4$ cup chopped onion
3 mushrooms, sliced

$1^1/2$ teaspoons extra virgin olive oil
$1/2$ cup tomato sauce
1 ounce grated Parmesan cheese or crumbled feta

Preheat oven to 425 degrees. Bake the polenta squares on an oiled tray for 5 minutes on each side. The polenta is done when it starts to bubble and the edges look crisp.

Meanwhile, in a medium skillet, sauté the onions and mushrooms in the oil. In a small saucepan, warm the tomato sauce. Using a metal spatula, slip a warm polenta square onto a dinner plate. Top with the tomato sauce and then top that with the mushroom and onion mixture. Sprinkle the cheese over the top.

Kasha Tabouli

Buckwheat is outstanding used in place of the usual cracked wheat in this Middle Eastern salad. Because buckwheat contains little gluten, it is a good substitute for people allergic to wheat, which does contain gluten. Use whole buckwheat groats and take care to cook them al dente so you get a fluffy, light salad that is not mushy.

Pinch sea salt
1 cup whole kasha (toasted buckwheat groats)
2 tablespoons chopped fresh mint
1 clove garlic, pressed or minced
1/2 cup chopped fresh parsley
1 teaspoon chopped fresh basil

1 large tomato, seeded and chopped
1/4 cup fresh-squeezed lemon juice
2 tablespoons natural soy sauce
1/4 cup extra virgin olive oil
Whole lettuce leaves, for garnish
1/4 cup pitted and halved black Greek olives, for garnish

In a small pot, bring 2 cups water to a boil, add the sea salt and the kasha. Cover, reduce heat, and simmer 20 minutes or until all the water is absorbed. Let the grain cool, then place all ingredients except the lettuce leaves and olives in a bowl and toss together lightly. Chill for an hour or more to allow flavors to blend. Line a salad bowl with the lettuce leaves. Fill bowl with the tabouli and garnish with the olives.

Kasha and Onion Piroshki

MAKES 16 PIROSHKI

Crisp whole-wheat pastry is the perfect foil for the velvety texture and Russian flavors of the filling in these small stuffed pastries. Instead of high-fat sour cream, we use vinegar to provide a rich flavor for the sauce to serve on the side. Serve piroshki with a bowl of Tangy Borscht (page 29) for a warming winter meal.

FILLING
1 tablespoon corn oil
2 cups finely chopped onion
1 tablespoon natural soy sauce

1 cup whole kasha
1 cup well-drained sauerkraut

PASTRY
2 cups whole-wheat flour
2 cups unbleached white flour

½ cup corn oil
½ teaspoon sea salt

For filling: Heat the oil in a skillet and add onions and sauté until partially tender, about 5 minutes. In a small saucepan bring 2 cups water and the soy sauce to a boil. Add the kasha to the onions and stir, then add the boiling soy and water. When the mixture returns to a boil, reduce the heat to low. Cook, covered, until all the liquid is absorbed, about 15 minutes. Mix in sauerkraut. Set in strainer and press to remove excess liquid. Be sure filling is at room temperature before using.

For pastry: In a large bowl, mix together the flours, oil, salt, and 1 cup water until it forms a dough. Knead briefly until smooth. Add a little more flour or water if necessary. Divide dough into eight equal portions. Roll out thin, and trim to 5-inch-square shape.

Preheat oven to 400 degrees. Place ¼ cup filling in center of each pastry square. Bring corners to center to barely overlap. Pinch newly formed corners together. Turn squares over and place on oiled baking sheet, seam side down, to bake until underside is barely golden, about 12 minutes. Serve warm.

3. Pasta

Eating well often requires making choices. When it comes to pasta, there are trade-offs between taste and nutrition that complicate choices for people committed to eating a diet of whole foods and good taste.

Everyone loves the nutty flavor and perfect texture of golden semolina pasta. Unfortunately, it's easy to forget that this is a refined food. To make it, durum wheat is stripped of its nutrient-rich bran and germ layers. When this wheat is made into semolina flour for making pasta, it is often fortified to put back part of what is removed in processing. However, the lost fiber, minerals, and some vitamins are not replaced.

Your other option is whole-wheat pasta. Made with the whole grain, it retains all the nutrients of high-protein durum wheat. However, whole-wheat pastas crack easily when cooked and have an assertive flavor. Finding dishes in which the strong taste of whole-wheat pasta blends harmoniously with the flavors of the other ingredients and in which its texture does not stand out awkwardly is difficult.

We've taken up the challenge of creating pasta dishes you'll like because we feel that in a sensible diet, there's room for all kinds of pasta. Some recipes use conventional durum semolina pasta. Some use whole-wheat pasta, or wheat-free pastas, such as buckwheat, that are useful for people allergic to wheat or gluten. If you are concerned about avoiding wheat, look for pasta made from rice, corn, legumes, even wild rice. Here are some of the many kinds of pastas available in natural food stores and an increasing number of supermarkets, where you may find them in either the natural food or ethnic sections.

KAMUT AND SPELT—Ancient forms of wheat that are higher in lipids and amino acids than durum wheat. Their higher fat content makes these whole-grain pastas more supple than those made from whole durum wheat. Some people who cannot tolerate wheat are able to eat pastas made from either of these grains.

SOBA—Thin beige Japanese noodles made using buckwheat. They may be a combination of wheat and buckwheat flour. The more buckwheat soba noodles contain, the more fragile they are when cooked, and the more they cost. When cooking these strong-tasting noodles, start them in cold water. When the water boils, pour in more cold water and bring to a boil again. The cooling and reheating process allows the inside of the noodles time to cook while preventing the outside from becoming mushy. Rinse cooked soba noodles in cold water immediately after draining or they will clump together. In Japan, soba are served both hot in soups, and cold accompanied by a dipping sauce.

FARRO—It is not clear if this Italian grain is related more closely to ancient strains of wheat or to buckwheat, which is a member of the rhubarb family. Farro makes a dark, sweet-tasting, firm-textured pasta. Imported *pasta di farro* is sold in Italian and specialty food stores.

PIZZOCHERI—Flat buckwheat noodles made in the Valtellina region of Italy. They are used to make a hearty baked dish, also called *Pizzocheri,* in which the noodles are layered together with dark greens, potatoes, and cheese. Look for *pizzocheri* at Italian and specialty food stores.

JERUSALEM ARTICHOKE—Pasta made from a combination of this vegetable and durum semolina. It can be eaten by some people who cannot tolerate wheat. These pastas taste like those made from regular semolina and have the same good texture. Jerusalem artichoke pasta is often sold in supermarkets as well as in natural food stores.

Convenience aside, pasta would still win popularity contests because it is low in fat and high in complex carbohydrates. Take advantage of this by making pasta in ways that do not load on fat through sauces or other added ingredients. Instead, see how well pasta combines with vegetables and legumes that add fiber and flavors to make dishes that taste good with the addition of just a minimum amount of butter or oil.

Japanese Fried Noodles

All the flavors typical of Japanese cooking meld in the sauce for this dish. *Mirin* is a wine made with sweet and malted rice. It adds sweetness without refined sugar. The balance of sweet, salty, sour, and bitter in the sauce makes it delicious on stir-fried vegetables as well as on pasta. Serve with Avocado Sashimi (page 202).

3 tablespoons sweet white miso	1 tablespoon dark sesame oil
2 tablespoons mirin	1 tablespoon sesame oil
2 tablespoons natural soy sauce	2 tablespoons minced shallots
8 ounces udon noodles	Slivered scallions, for garnish

In a small bowl, combine the miso, *mirin,* and natural soy sauce and set aside.

In a large pot, bring 8 cups water to a boil. Add the *udon* and cook until the noodles are al dente, according to package directions. Immediately drain and rinse under cold running water. Drain again and toss with the dark sesame oil.

In a large skillet, heat the sesame oil over medium heat. Add the shallots and sauté 1 minute. Add the noodles, raise heat to medium-high, and sauté briefly. Add the miso mixture, and toss to coat the noodles evenly. If the sauce evaporates and becomes too concentrated, add a little water. Cook 1 minute more, then remove from heat. Serve immediately with a generous sprinkling of scallions.

Linguini Aglio e Olio

Of all the healing foods, garlic is perhaps the oldest and best known. It can help lower blood serum cholesterol and decrease the likelihood of the formation of blood clots, and it has anti-cancer properties. The technique of sautéing garlic in oil is one of the simplest ways to incorporate garlic into your cooking, as in this classic pasta dish. Serve with a green salad.

8 ounces linguine, *or* udon *noodles*
2 tablespoons extra virgin olive oil
3 large cloves garlic, minced

Sea salt to taste
3 tablespoons minced fresh parsley
¼ cup grated Parmesan cheese

In a large pot of salted boiling water, cook linguini or *udon* until al dente, according to package directions.

While pasta is cooking, in a large skillet over medium-low heat, heat the oil. Add the garlic and cook briefly; make sure it doesn't brown or it will taste bitter.

When pasta is done, drain, allowing some water to cling to the strands. Mix the dripping pasta with the oil and garlic. Add salt to taste, and parsley. Toss to mix well. Sprinkle on the grated Parmesan cheese; serve immediately.

VARIATION: Add one or more vegetables—such as broccoli or cauliflower florets, snow peas or sugar snap peas, sliced carrots, zucchini, or asparagus. The vegetables should be blanched in boiling water until just tender-crisp, drained, then tossed in the oil and garlic just before adding pasta.

Fettuccine with Wild Mushrooms and Herbs

This is an easy way to enjoy the delicious flavors of fresh porcini, shiitake, oyster, chanterelle, or Cremini mushrooms. While they are quite costly, their flavors are so intense that you can mix them with one another and with less expensive white mushrooms; use one kind or any combination of mushrooms and you will still have a wonderful dish. Mushrooms release liquid as they cook. In this recipe, instead of being cooked away, this flavorful liquid becomes the base of the sauce. Fresh herbs and garlic bring out the earthy flavor of the mushrooms.

2 tablespoons extra virgin olive oil
1/2 cup thinly sliced onion (about 1 small onion)
4 large cloves garlic, minced
4 cups thinly sliced mushrooms (about 1/2 pound)

1 teaspoon dried oregano
1/8 teaspoon dried rosemary
1 teaspoon sea salt
Pinch black pepper
1/2 pound fettuccine
Parsley, for garnish

In a skillet, heat the oil over medium heat, add the onion and garlic, and sauté until the onions are translucent, about 5 minutes. Add the mushrooms, oregano, rosemary, salt, and pepper. Stir, cover, and cook about 10 minutes, stirring briefly once or twice.

Meanwhile, in a large pot of salted boiling water, cook pasta al dente, according to package directions. Drain and turn into a large bowl.

Spoon the mushroom mixture over the pasta and toss gently. Garnish with parsley and serve immediately.

Linguini with Dark Greens and Beans

Few cooks prepare dark, leafy greens as beautifully as the Italians. This hearty dish is typical of Italian country cooking. It works well with chicory or young, tender dandelion greens, but almost any leafy green, or broccoli florets, can be substituted. Leafy greens are rich in beta carotene, vitamin C, and other substances that may help protect against cancer. Plus, they are good sources of iron and even calcium.

3 tablespoons extra virgin olive oil
3 cloves garlic, minced
1 large bunch leafy greens, chopped;
  1 large head chicory, chopped; or
  1 bunch broccoli, separated into florets
1/4 teaspoon sea salt

Pinch white pepper
1/2 teaspoon dried marjoram
1 (15-ounce) can chick-peas, or Great
  Northern beans, drained and rinsed
1/2 pound linguini

Bring a large pot of salted water to a boil. Cook pasta al dente, about 8–10 minutes or according to package directions.

In a large skillet, heat 2 tablespoons of oil over low heat and cook the garlic 1 minute. Add the chopped greens or broccoli florets, cook briefly, then add the salt, pepper, and marjoram, and 1/2 cup of water. Cover and cook 4–5 minutes. Add the beans, toss, cover, and gently simmer until the greens or broccoli are just tender, 3–5 minutes more.

Drain pasta allowing some water to cling to the strands. While still dripping wet, toss pasta with remaining 1 tablespoon of oil.

Toss the vegetable-bean mixture with the linguine, add more salt to taste, if needed, and serve hot.

Pasta with Green Olives and Avocado

Avocado makes a light, buttery counterpoint to the intense, briny flavor of the olives in this unusual dish. Avocados are exceptionally rich in potassium and are also a good source of beta carotene. Serve this pasta as a first course, either warm or at room temperature.

8 ounces spaghetti or fettuccine
3 tablespoons extra virgin olive oil
1 clove garlic, minced
1/4 teaspoon dried marjoram

1/2 cup pitted and sliced green olives
1 small ripe avocado, peeled, pitted, and sliced thin

Preheat oven to 200 degrees. In a large pot of salted boiling water, cook pasta al dente, according to package directions.

While pasta is cooking, put 1 tablespoon of the oil in a large ovenproof bowl and warm it in the oven. Mix the remaining 2 tablespoons of oil with the garlic, marjoram, olives, and avocado. When the pasta is done, drain, and while dripping wet, toss it with the olive oil in the heated bowl. Add the olive mixture, toss, and serve.

Pasta Primavera

The creamy sauce on this colorful pasta dish is dairy-free. In place of cream, which is high in cholesterol, tahini, a paste made of ground sesame seeds, adds richness to the sauce. Since sesame seeds are a good source of calcium, you get the same benefits as if dairy products had been used as well as the goodness of mono- and polyunsaturated oils. Vary the vegetables in this dish to your taste, perhaps using green peas, string beans, or cauliflower florets, but be careful not to overcook them; they should be tender-crisp.

2 cups broccoli florets
2 cups julienne carrots
1 cup fresh or frozen corn kernels (1 large ear)
1½ tablespoons extra virgin olive oil
2 cloves garlic, minced
½ cup diced onion (about ½ medium onion)
3 tablespoons whole-wheat flour
2 cups Basic Vegetable Stock (page 21), plus additional for thinning sauce

Pinch sea salt
Pinch white pepper
2 tablespoons natural soy sauce
2 tablespoons mellow white miso
2 tablespoons tahini
3 tablespoons finely chopped fresh basil
¼ cup minced fresh parsley, plus extra for garnish
1 tablespoon red wine vinegar, or fresh lemon juice
8 ounces macaroni, rotelli, or shells

Fill a large pot with water and bring it to a boil. Blanch the broccoli florets 4–5 minutes and remove with a slotted spoon. In the same pot, blanch the carrots 2 minutes and remove, then blanch the corn 2 minutes and remove. Combine the vegetables in a bowl and cover with foil to keep them warm.

In a medium skillet over low heat, heat the oil and cook the garlic and onion 1 minute. Be careful not to brown the garlic or it will taste bitter. Add the flour and stir constantly for 1 minute. Slowly add the stock, whisking until sauce thickens. Add salt and pepper, and simmer 5 minutes, adding a little more stock if the sauce gets too thick. (It should be about the consistency of heavy cream.)

In a small bowl, combine the soy sauce, miso, and tahini. Gradually mix in ¼ cup of water, or additional stock. Add the mixture to the thickened sauce and simmer gently 2 minutes. Add the basil, parsley, and vinegar or lemon juice and cook 1 minute longer. Pour the sauce over vegetables and toss gently.

Meanwhile, in a large pot of salted boiling water, cook the pasta al dente according to package directions, drain, and return to pot. Immediately add the sauce mixture. Toss gently, and serve with a sprinkling of parsley.

Spaghetti with Shrimp Sauce

Here is a seafood lover's dream. Although higher in cholesterol than most seafood, shrimp is low in fat and calories and is a good source of vitamin B$_{12}$ and zinc. The concentrated essence of the shrimp stock makes this dish sing with sweet flavor. Mushrooms add depth, and arrowroot gives the sauce a creamy texture. Serve with a side dish of steamed greens.

³/₄ pound medium shrimp in the shell

STOCK
Shells of shrimp
1 whole clove garlic, unpeeled

SAUCE
3 tablespoons extra virgin olive oil
2–3 cloves garlic, minced
1 cup finely chopped onion (about 1 medium onion)
8 ounces mushrooms, stems removed, caps cut into wedges
¹/₂ cup dry white wine
³/₄ cup reserved strained stock

Pinch sea salt

2 sprigs parsley

Sea salt to taste
Reserved shrimp
¹/₄ teaspoon black pepper
¹/₄ cup chopped fresh parsley
1 tablespoon arrowroot dissolved in 1 tablespoon cold water
³/₄ pound linguine, or spaghetti

For stock: Shell and devein the shrimp. In a bowl, toss the shrimp with a pinch of salt, and set aside.

In a small saucepan, combine the shells, garlic, and parsley with just enough water to cover and bring to a boil. Reduce heat, cover, and simmer 20 minutes. Strain and discard the shells, garlic, and parsley.

For sauce: In a saucepan over low heat, heat 2 tablespoons of the olive oil and sauté the garlic and onion 1–2 minutes. Be careful not to brown the garlic, or it will taste bitter. Raise the heat to medium. Add the mushrooms and sauté 1 minute, stirring constantly. Add the wine, ¾ cup of the strained stock, sea salt to taste, and the pepper. Lower heat and simmer sauce gently, uncovered, 3 minutes. Add the shrimp, and simmer for 3 minutes. Add the parsley, reserving a little for garnish.

Add the arrowroot mixture to the shrimp mixture, stirring briskly until sauce is thickened. Remove from heat.

For pasta: In a large pot of boiling salted water, cook the pasta al dente, according to package directions. Drain pasta and return to the pot. Immediately add the remaining tablespoon of oil and toss to coat the pasta.

To serve: Add the shrimp with its sauce to pot with cooked pasta. Toss, and serve hot, topped with a sprinkling of reserved chopped parsley.

Green Bean and Macaroni Salad

Combining beans and grains is the optimum way to obtain high-quality vegetable protein. Together, these foods supply complementary amino acids and provide a complete vegetable protein. This simple and delicious salad can be a meal in itself, or serve it with fresh corn on the cob or other summer favorites. It is great for potlucks and picnics.

8 ounces macaroni
7 ounces green beans cut (1-inch lengths), about 2 cups
1 cucumber, peeled
2 cups cooked and drained chick-peas, or kidney beans
5 scallions, sliced thin

3 red radishes, halved, then sliced into thin half-moons
1/3 cup sliced pitted black olives, or chopped dill pickles
1 tablespoon finely chopped fresh basil
1/3 cup mellow white miso
3 tablespoons brown rice vinegar

In a large pot of boiling salted water, cook the pasta al dente, according to package directions. Drain, rinse under cold water to cool, and drain again.

Meanwhile, blanch the green beans in boiling water until tender-crisp and still bright green, about 5 minutes. Drain and cool. Quarter the cucumber lengthwise, scoop out seeds, and slice thinly crosswise.

In a large bowl, toss the cooked macaroni with the green beans, cucumber, chick-peas or kidney beans, scallions, radishes, olives or pickles, and basil. In a small bowl, combine the miso and vinegar with 5 tablespoons of water. Add to the macaroni mixture, stir to blend well, and serve.

Spicy Soba Noodle Salad

Soba noodles are the easiest way to enjoy the goodness of buckwheat, which is a valuable source of minerals, including magnesium and manganese. It is important to rinse these noodles immediately after they are drained; otherwise they become a sticky mass. Vary the vegetables according to what is in season. Fresh peas, corn, red and green pepper, and radish are colorful options. Serve with Avocado Sashimi (page 202) for a nice, light meal.

1 cup carrots (cut in matchsticks $1/2$ inch long, about $1/2$ pound)
$1^{1}/2$ cups broccoli florets
8 ounces soba noodles
2 scallions, thinly sliced
2 tablespoons minced fresh parsley

1 tablespoon sesame oil
1 tablespoon dark sesame oil
2 tablespoons natural soy sauce
$1/4$ teaspoon sea salt
3 tablespoons brown rice vinegar
1 clove garlic, minced

In a large pot of boiling water, blanch the carrots 1–2 minutes, remove with slotted spoon, rinse under cold water, and drain. In the same water, blanch the broccoli 3–4 minutes. Remove, rinse under cold water, drain, and set aside.

Break the noodles into three or four even lengths. In large pot of salted boiling water, cook soba al dente, about 5 minutes, and drain. Immediately cool under running water, then drain again.

In a large bowl, combine the noodles, carrots, broccoli, scallions, and parsley. In a small bowl, whisk together the remaining ingredients, and pour over the noodle mixture. Toss gently and serve.

Angel-Hair Pasta with Grilled Tomato-Basil Sauce

SERVES 4

This dish demands vine-ripened, fresh tomatoes. Grilling enriches their bold taste, while the sweetness of the onions softens their acid edge. No salt is called for in this recipe; in our opinion, this dish has big, full flavor without it. Serve with grilled garlic bread and a fresh garden salad.

 12 *ripe tomatoes, halved*
  3 *medium onions, peeled and halved*
  6 *tablespoons extra virgin olive oil*
12–16 *ounces angel-hair pasta*
 ½ *cup chopped fresh basil*

 ½ *cup chopped fresh parsley*
  1 *tablespoon minced garlic*
 ½ *teaspoon red pepper flakes*
 ½ *cup grated Parmesan or soy cheese*

Brush the tomato and onion halves lightly with 2 tablespoons of the oil. Over medium heat, grill until browned, 8–10 minutes. Remove from the grill, discard tomato skins, and chop both vegetables coarsely.

In a large pot of salted boiling water, cook the pasta al dente, according to package directions. Drain the pasta and place in a large bowl. Add the basil, parsley, remaining oil, garlic, and pepper flakes, and toss well. Add the chopped tomatoes and onions, toss, and serve with the grated cheese.

Fresh Corn, Tofu, and Spiral Noodle Salad

SERVES 6–8

This salad, which includes a grain, a bean, and vegetables, makes a balanced light lunch. Parsley is so often a mere garnish in recipes, but here its aromatic flavor is an important element. It also adds a major nutrient boost. Just 1 ounce of parsley contains 43 percent of the RDA for vitamin C and 18 percent of the RDA for iron for men (12 percent for women). Serve with Cucumber Tomato Salad (page 143) for a light supper.

$1^1/_2$ cups fresh or frozen corn kernels (2 medium ears)
$1^1/_2$ pounds tofu
2 cups chopped fresh parsley (about 2 bunches)
1 cup chopped scallions (about 6 scallions)
8 ounces whole-wheat spiral pasta
$^1/_4$ cup extra virgin olive oil
3 tablespoons umeboshi *vinegar*

In a saucepan, steam the corn until done, about 7 minutes, and cool. Cut the tofu into five or six pieces, steam 5 minutes, and cool. In a large bowl, mash the cooled tofu with a fork. Add the corn, parsley, and scallions. Mix to blend and set aside.

Meanwhile, in large pot of salted boiling water, cook pasta al dente, according to package directions. Drain, rinse under cold running water, and drain again. Add corn-tofu mixture to pasta and mix to blend.

In a small bowl, combine oil and *umeboshi* vinegar, and sprinkle on pasta mixture. Toss together lightly and serve.

4. Seitan, Tempeh, and Tofu

How can you get protein into a meal when you are not using meat, fish, or dairy products? Grains and legumes are both good sources of protein. Along with obvious choices from these food groups, including pasta and beans, you can also use tempeh, tofu, and seitan. Over the years, we have helped *Natural Health* readers discover these versatile, high-protein foods.

Tempeh and tofu are made from soybeans. Seitan, also called *wheat meat,* is the gluten—the protein component—of wheat. These three foods originated in Asia, where they have been a staple source of protein and other nutrients for centuries.

SEITAN

Meat eaters who try this chewy meat analogue tell us how much they enjoy it. Seitan is made by kneading wheat flour into a stiff dough to develop the gluten in the flour. This dough is rinsed under running water until all the starch and bran have washed away, leaving only the spongelike protein, or gluten. Cooking in a broth firms the seitan and enhances its mildly nutty taste. While home cooks can make seitan, most people prefer buying it already cooked and ready to use. Look for it, in its cooking broth, in tubs in the refrigerator section, or in jars on the shelves of natural food stores.

In addition to its pleasing texture and agreeable flavor, seitan has the virtue of being fat-free. The best way to use it is in stews and stir-fries.

SOY FOODS

Soybeans are more than just a powerhouse of protein. They are the only legume whose proteins are considered complete. That means they contain all essential amino acids, including lysine, methionine, cystine, threonine, and tryptophan, needed to supply 100 percent of the daily requirements. They are also high in fiber and a good source of complex carbohydrates. Soybeans are relatively high in fat but 85 percent of it is unsaturated fatty acids.

Most of the U.S. soybean crop is used for animal feed and to make industrial products. In Asia, the soybean could be called the "green cow." Asians use it to make protein-rich tempeh, tofu, and a beverage commonly referred to as *soy milk*. Soybeans are also sprouted and used to make a myriad of soy sauces; they are also fermented to make miso, a flavorful bean paste.

Tempeh

The yeasty fullness of tempeh puts it close to meat in flavor. This soy food originated in Indonesia. It is made by injecting partially cooked, coarsely chopped soybeans with *Rhizopus oligosporus* bacteria, which produces mycelium, white fibers that bind the soybeans into a cake. Because of the fermentation in this process, tempeh is exceptionally high in protein, and these proteins are particularly digestible. It is also the only vegetable food that contains vitamin B_{12}, although not in a form that the body can use. When culturing is completed, the tempeh is cut into flat cakes and vacuum-packed. Look for it in the refrigerated case at natural food stores. Tempeh can be made solely from soybeans, or can include rice, millet, or barley, or a combination of grains with the soybeans. Soy tempeh has the most pronounced, mushroomy flavor and is also higher in protein and fat than the blended kinds.

The best ways to cook tempeh are by grilling or frying. Fried, cubed tempeh can be added to stews, mashed into spreads, or topped with a sauce.

Tofu

You have probably tried tofu. You may find it subtly flavored and pleasant, or mushy and bland. Actually, this soy food is so versatile that there are many ways to use it: cubed, steamed, and topped with a sauce; added to stews or stir-fries; fried; mashed into a spread; pureed for a dip; or used in a cheese cake.

Tofu is made from the milk pressed from pureed, cooked soybeans. A coagulant—traditionally *nigari* (magnesium chloride), but calcium sulfate or calcium chloride are also used—is added, just as rennet is added to warm milk in cheesemaking. If there is calcium in the coagulant, the tofu will also be a rich source of calcium. When the coagulated liquid has separated into curds and whey, the curds are drained and pressed into blocks of tofu. Depending on the amount of water pressed out, the tofu produced is soft as custard, firm, or extra-firm. Use the firmest kinds for stir-fries and other main dishes, and try the softer ones for making dips, desserts, and toppings such as Tofu Sour Cream (page 163).

Some recipes in this book call for pressed tofu. Pressing firms tofu, giving it a chewier texture. To press tofu, place a block of it on several layers of paper toweling. Add more paper towels on top, then a plate, heavy skillet, or small cutting board. Place a weight on top of this. Cans of tomatoes or several bags of dried beans work nicely. When the towels become soaked with liquid from the tofu, change them and replace the weights. Repeat this once or twice, depending on how firm you want the tofu to be.

NOTE: When a recipe calls for using tofu in a dish that will not be cooked, blanch the tofu for 2–3 minutes to kill any possible bacterial growth, then combine with other ingredients. Treat tofu as you would animal foods. If it is to be marinated, always do so in the refrigerator to prevent the growth of unwanted bacteria.

Other Soy Foods

Miso, a savory fermented soybean paste that originated in China 2,500 years ago, is a common ingredient in Asian cooking. Soybeans are combined with salt, water, and *koji,* which is a culture of *Aspergillus oryzae* bacteria. This mixture is allowed to sit until the bacteria have done their work and the beans have become a velvety paste, a process that takes from two months to three years. Japanese and natural food stores carry several kinds of miso. Darker, red misos are aged longer and taste saltier than white and yellow misos, which are sweeter. Read the label on the pale misos, because some of them are bleached and contain preservatives.

Recipes generally call for only a few tablespoons of miso. Even this amount contributes useful amounts of protein, B vitamins, and minerals, and enhances digestion. Using miso in moderation is important, particularly if you are on a sodium-restricted diet, as it is very high in sodium.

Soy sauce, a by-product of making miso, is a salty liquid pressed out of the fermented bean paste, then aged. Naturally fermented soy sauce consists of soybeans, wheat, water, and salt, and takes about two years to make. During aging, complex flavors develop; quick-fermented soy sauces have less depth of flavor. Some soy sauce is not fermented at all. Ingredients for these inferior products include hydrolyzed vegetable protein, soy extract, caramel coloring, salt, water, and corn syrup. To tell what quality of soy sauce you are getting, it's important to read the label. Some soy sauces are called *shoyu* and others *tamari:* generally, shoyu is made with wheat, and tamari without. When looking at low-sodium soy sauces, keep in mind that they are still quite high in sodium.

Soy beverage (also called soy milk) is a pale beige liquid that is pressed from ground soybeans, cooked, and filtered. Soy beverage has more protein and less fat and calcium than cow's milk, though some soy beverages are now fortified with calcium to compensate for this. Use this liquid as you would milk, avoiding the flavored kinds when cooking, except in some desserts. When soy beverage is heated, it turns dark or grayish; it tastes fine but can look unappetizing in sauces or puddings. Soy beverage is sold in aseptic boxes on the shelves of supermarkets and natural food stores. It is also sold fresh in the refrigerated cases in some natural food stores and Asian markets.

Seitan Stroganoff

Here's a creamy, flavorful dish you can put together quickly. Prepare the ingredients in the morning and then make up this dairy-free Stroganoff at dinnertime while the noodles are cooking. Serve with Tofu Sour Cream.

8 ounces linguine, or flat noodles
3 tablespoons extra virgin olive oil
2 tablespoons minced garlic
2 cups seitan, cut into thin, bite-size
   pieces
8 ounces sliced fresh mushrooms (3 cups)
1/4 teaspoon sea salt

1/8 teaspoon black pepper
1/4 teaspoon dried marjoram
1/4 teaspoon dried basil
1/4 cup dry white wine
1 cup Tofu Sour Cream (page 163)
1 tablespoon minced fresh parsley

Cook noodles al dente, according to package directions. Drain and, while still dripping wet, toss with 1 tablespoon of the oil.

In a skillet, heat 1 tablespoon of the oil over medium-low heat, and sauté the garlic until translucent, about 1 minute. Add the seitan, and sauté just until brown on both sides, a few minutes. Remove the garlic and seitan from the pan.

Add the remaining tablespoon of oil to the pan, and sauté the mushrooms with the salt 2–3 minutes. Return the garlic and seitan to the pan, add the pepper, marjoram, and basil, and toss. Add the wine and stir just to mix. Heat briefly, and gently add the Tofu Sour Cream to warm. Do not cook or the Tofu Sour Cream will separate.

Divide the noodles among two or three plates, top with Stroganoff, sprinkle with parsley, and serve.

Seitan Pot Pie

Corn adds a fresh touch to this meatless version of an American classic. The arrowroot and *kuzu* (both unrefined thickeners) give the filling a creamy consistency. *Mirin* plus an egg yolk add delicious richness. Plan to make this dish the day you serve it, since refrigerating affects the texture of the filling.

FILLING

4 tablespoons sesame oil
1 pound seitan, cut into bite-size cubes and drained
1/3 cup arrowroot
1 clove garlic, minced
1 cup chopped onion (1 medium onion)
1 cup diced carrots (2–3 carrots)
1 cup diced potatoes (1 medium potato)
3 tablespoons mirin
1/4 cup natural soy sauce

1/4 teaspoon black pepper
1/2 teaspoon dried sage
1/2 teaspoon dried thyme
1 1/2 teaspoons kuzu *dissolved in 3 tablespoons water*
1 egg yolk beaten with 2 tablespoons plain soy beverage
1 cup fresh or frozen corn kernels (1 large ear)
1 cup green peas

CRUST

1 cup whole-wheat pastry flour, chilled
1/2 cup unbleached white flour, chilled
1/4 teaspoon sea salt

1/3 cup corn oil, chilled
3–4 tablespoons ice water
1 egg, beaten lightly

For filling: In a heavy skillet, heat 3 tablespoons of the oil. Dredge the seitan pieces in arrowroot and drop into the hot oil. Sauté, turning as necessary, about 4 minutes, until the seitan is crispy and the arrowroot coating is golden brown. Drain on paper towels.

In a clean skillet, heat the remaining tablespoon of the oil, and cook the garlic and onion until translucent, about 5 minutes. Add the carrots and potatoes, and continue cooking until partially tender, a few more minutes. Pour in the *mirin* and enough water just to cover the vegetables. Bring to a boil, reduce heat, and allow the stew to simmer until tender, but not mushy, about 5 minutes. Season to taste with soy sauce, black pepper, sage, and thyme. Add the dissolved *kuzu* slowly to the stew. Bring mixture to a gentle boil, stirring continuously. Cook until the stew thickens, about 2 minutes. Blend a few spoonfuls of the hot liquid into the egg yolk and soy mixture and then stir this mixture into the filling. Stir in the corn kernels, peas, and seitan cubes.

Pour the mixture into a lightly oiled pie plate and allow to cool while making crust.

For crust: Preheat oven to 375 degrees. In a large bowl, sift the flours together with the salt. Add the oil and blend with a fork until the dough is a coarse meal. Add the water, a tablespoon at a time. Stop as soon as the dough pulls away from the sides of the bowl and forms a ball. Do not overmix. Do not knead. Wrap dough in waxed paper. Chill in refrigerator 30 minutes.

Run a damp sponge over a cutting board or work surface, and place on it a piece of waxed paper that is 3 inches larger than your pie plate. Flatten the pie dough into a disk and lay it on the waxed paper, then lay another sheet of waxed paper over the dough. Working from the center out toward the edges, roll the dough to ½–⅛-inch thick and about 2 inches larger than the pie plate.

Peel off the top paper and, using the bottom paper to pick up the dough, flip it onto the filling in the pie plate. Peel off the waxed paper. The dough should hang over the edges of the pan. Moisten the edges, fold them under, and flute. Decoratively prick or slash the top of the crust to allow steam to escape. Brush the crust with the egg and bake until the crust is golden brown, 30–35 minutes. Cool slightly, about 10 minutes, before cutting.

Sweet and Sour Red Cabbage with Seitan

Meat eaters will not even notice what's missing from this satisfying German-style dish. The combination of vinegars helps the cabbage keep its bright color. Baking melds the flavors of the cabbage, apple, and seasonings. Serve with boiled potatoes.

1 *pound seitan*
  Canola oil for deep-frying
1 *tablespoon extra virgin olive oil*
6 *cups finely shredded red cabbage*
3 *cups chopped onion (3 medium onions)*

3 *sweet apples, peeled, cored, and slivered*
2 *tablespoons* umeboshi *vinegar*
2 *tablespoons balsamic vinegar*
1 *tablespoon caraway seeds*
  Parsley, for garnish

Squeeze seitan gently to remove excess liquid, cut into 1½-inch pieces, and deep-fry in 2 inches of hot canola oil just until the outsides are crisp. Drain on paper towels.

Preheat oven to 350 degrees. In a large skillet over medium heat, heat the olive oil, and sauté the cabbage and onion until cabbage has wilted and onions are transparent, 5–10 minutes. Add the apples and sauté 1 minute longer, then add the vinegars and caraway seeds.

Place cabbage mixture in a large ovenproof dish with lid, cover, and bake. After 20 minutes bury the seitan pieces in the mixture, then bake 20 minutes longer. Garnish with parsley and serve.

Snow Peas with Shiitake Mushrooms and Seitan

The earthy flavors of the mushrooms and burdock in this warming dish are just right on a cold winter day. Nutritionally, shiitakes have antiviral properties. Burdock is a strengthening food that helps to hasten recovery from illness, so keep this recipe ready during cold and flu season. Serve with brown rice and Parsnips in Sweet Miso (page 97).

2–3 *teaspoons sesame oil*
2 *medium onions, cut in half, then sliced thin in half-moons*
8 *ounces seitan, thinly sliced*
1 *cup peeled and thinly sliced burdock*
3 *teaspoons natural soy sauce*
10 *dried shiitake mushrooms, soaked in water to cover for 1 hour, with soaking water reserved*

3 *cups thinly sliced Chinese cabbage*
1 *cup stemmed, threaded, and diagonally sliced snow peas (¹/₂-inch pieces)*

In a 2- or 3-quart pot, heat the oil and cook the onions until translucent, 3–5 minutes. Add the seitan, burdock, and soy sauce, and cook 5 more minutes.

Squeeze excess water from shiitakes. Remove the stems (which can be reserved for a stock), and chop the mushroom caps fine. Add the mushrooms and ¹/₂ cup of the soaking water to the seitan mixture. Reduce heat, cover tightly, and simmer 30 minutes. Add water if needed. Add the Chinese cabbage and snow peas. Cover and let the green vegetables cook until done but crisp, 2–3 minutes.

French-style Braised Tempeh

Herbs and red wine give this hearty dish the deep flavors of a rustic bourguignon. The lemon zest adds an unexpected, aromatic touch. Serve this dish with a green salad and noodles for a festive meal.

1/2 cup canola oil
12 ounces tempeh, cut into 12 pieces
2 teaspoons olive oil
1 large onion, diced
2 cloves garlic, minced, plus 1 whole clove, peeled
3/4 teaspoon dried basil
1/2 teaspoon dried thyme
1/4 teaspoon dried oregano
1/2 teaspoon ground cumin
1/4 teaspoon ground coriander
1/4 teaspoon ground fennel
1 bay leaf
1 clove
1 cup dry red wine
1 × 3-inch-strip lemon zest
1 tablespoon natural soy sauce
1/2 teaspoon Dijon mustard, or to taste

In a skillet, heat the canola oil over medium heat and lightly brown the pieces of tempeh on all sides, about 10 minutes. Remove to paper towels to drain.

In a clean pan, heat the olive oil and cook the onion and minced garlic until browned, about 15 minutes. Add the basil, thyme, oregano, cumin, coriander, fennel, and bay leaf; cook 30 seconds longer, stirring continuously.

Stick the clove into the remaining garlic clove. Add that, plus the wine, lemon zest, soy sauce, and reserved tempeh to the pan. Add just enough water to cover. Bring to a boil and reduce the heat to a high simmer. Cook 30 minutes, turning the tempeh halfway through. If the water level falls, add more water.

Remove the tempeh to a warm plate. Discard the whole garlic, bay leaf, and lemon zest. Stir the mustard into the cooking liquid, and spoon the sauce over the tempeh. Serve hot, with steamed vegetables on rice.

Tempeh Shepherd's Pie

The English make this dish with leftover lamb. Brewer's yeast, barley malt, and tomatoes give this meatless version all the flavor you could want. This dish keeps well in the refrigerator; you can make it 2 or 3 days before serving.

FILLING

2 tablespoons extra virgin olive oil

2 cloves garlic, minced

1 cup chopped onion (1 medium onion)

1 cup diced red bell pepper

8 ounces tempeh, cut in $\frac{1}{2}$-inch cubes

$1\frac{1}{2}$ tablespoons natural soy sauce

$\frac{1}{2}$ teaspoon dried sage

$\frac{1}{4}$ teaspoon dried thyme

$\frac{1}{4}$ teaspoon black pepper

3 tablespoons dry red wine

2 tablespoons brewer's yeast

1 tablespoon barley malt syrup

$\frac{3}{4}$ cup fresh or frozen corn kernels (about 1 medium ear)

2 cups skinned and seeded tomatoes (1 [16-ounce] can, drained, or 4 fresh tomatoes)

$\frac{1}{3}$ cup tomato juice

TOPPING

$1\frac{1}{2}$ pounds potatoes, peeled and boiled

$\frac{1}{2}$ cup plain soy beverage

$\frac{1}{2}$ teaspoon sea salt

$1\frac{1}{2}$ tablespoons corn oil

Chopped fresh parsley, for garnish

For filling: In a heavy saucepan, heat the oil and sauté the garlic and onion until translucent, about 5 minutes. Add the red pepper, reduce the heat, and continue to cook until tender, about 10 minutes. In a medium bowl, combine the tempeh cubes with the soy sauce, sage, thyme, black pepper, wine, yeast, and barley malt. Add this mixture to the onions and pepper and cook 5 minutes, stirring often. Stir in the corn kernels, tomatoes, and juice. Allow to simmer 15 minutes over a low flame. Remove from heat, and cool to room temperature.

For topping: Preheat oven to 350 degrees.

In a large bowl, using a potato masher or heavy fork, mash together the potatoes and the soy beverage, salt, and corn oil. Do not use a blender or food processor, because they will make the potatoes gummy.

Pour the filling into an oiled heat-proof serving dish. Spread mashed potatoes evenly over the filling. Cover with foil and bake for 30 minutes. Remove foil and continue to bake an additional 10 minutes, browning the top. Garnish with chopped parsley.

Indonesian Tempeh Satay with Hot Peanut Sauce

SERVES 8 AS APPETIZER, 4 AS ENTREE

What we call a *kebab,* Indonesians call a *satay.* Either way the aromatic spices in this dish go perfectly with tempeh. Serve these highly seasoned cubes on skewers or on a bed of plain rice. Sliced cucumbers or Raita (page 148) would make a refreshing complement.

8 bamboo skewers
1/4 cup natural soy sauce
1 1/2 tablespoons fresh lime juice
1 tablespoon barley malt syrup
1 tablespoon minced cilantro

1 teaspoon honey
1 clove garlic, minced
   Pinch freshly ground black pepper
8 ounces tempeh, cut into 1/2-inch cubes
2 tablespoons peanut oil

Soak the skewers in water at least 2 hours, or overnight. In a bowl, combine the soy sauce, lime juice, barley malt, cilantro, honey, garlic, and black pepper. Add the tempeh pieces, and marinate in the refrigerator several hours or overnight.

Slide tempeh pieces onto soaked skewers, spacing them so they are not touching. Grill over high heat until browned, about 5 minutes on each side, brushing with oil several times while grilling.

To serve as an appetizer, leave tempeh on skewers and accompany with small bowl of peanut sauce for dipping, or drizzle the sauce over the tempeh. To serve as a main course, slide tempeh off skewers onto a bed of rice and pour sauce on top.

VARIATION: Intersperse one or more of the following items between the marinated tempeh cubes before grilling: cherry tomatoes, small mushrooms, pearl onions, pineapple chunks, dates, prunes, or parboiled broccoli or cauliflower florets.

Hot Peanut Sauce

MAKES 3/4 CUP

Indonesians usually serve this thick, spiced sauce warm, but you can serve it at room temperature.

1/2 cup smooth peanut butter
1 scallion, chopped
1 clove garlic, minced
2 tablespoons fresh lemon juice

2 tablespoons natural soy sauce
1 teaspoon minced fresh ginger
1/8 teaspoon chili powder, or to taste

Place all ingredients in a blender or food processor, and process until smooth. If too thick, thin mixture with 1–2 tablespoons of water. Heat in a saucepan if desired.

Gingered Tempeh with Basil

Ginger is used extensively in the cuisines of Asia, being second in importance only to salt. Here it combines elegantly with deep-fried tempeh, oranges, and fragrant basil. Along with contributing appealing flavor to this unusual dish, the basil and ginger also encourage good digestion. Serve with an aromatic rice, such as white or brown basmati.

8 ounces tempeh
Safflower or canola oil for deep-frying
3 tablespoons natural soy sauce
5 slices fresh ginger, peeled
1 teaspoon dark sesame oil
1 medium onion, sliced into half-moons (about 1 cup)
1½ cups sliced mushrooms (4 ounces)
2 tablespoons chopped fresh basil, or ½ teaspoon dried

¼ teaspoon sea salt
1 cup thinly sliced carrots (sliced on the diagonal)
3 cups green beans (1-inch pieces, about 10 ounces)
2–3 teaspoons arrowroot dissolved in 1 tablespoon cold water
Orange slices and fresh parsley, for garnish

Cut the tempeh in half, forming two rectangles. Cut each rectangle on the diagonal to form four triangles. Cut each triangle in half horizontally to make two more triangles of the same area but with half the depth, totaling eight thin triangles.

In a skillet, heat oil 2 inches deep over moderate heat. To test whether it is hot enough, add a slice of tempeh. It should rise to the top of the oil a second or two after hitting the bottom of the pan. Deep-fry all the tempeh triangles until golden brown. Drain on paper towels.

In a large pot, bring 2 cups of water to a simmer. Add tempeh triangles, soy sauce, and ginger. Simmer 15 minutes. Remove the slices of ginger and discard. Set the cooked tempeh aside.

In a large skillet, heat the sesame oil over moderate heat. Add the onion, mushrooms, basil, and salt, and cook until onions are partially tender, about

3 minutes. Stir in the carrots and green beans. Add the tempeh and broth. Cover and cook 5 minutes.

Add the arrowroot mixture to the skillet and stir until the broth is thickened, about 3 minutes. Serve garnished with orange slices and parsley.

Black Pepper Tofu Steaks

SERVES 3

Tofu soaks up the flavor of the wine and spices in this zesty marinade in just an hour. Sear the tofu in a skillet or, better yet, cook it on a grill. Serve with Radish Rice Salad with Walnut Pesto Dressing (page 40) or Kasha Tabouli (page 51).

3 tablespoons natural soy sauce
3 tablespoons semi-dry white wine
3 cloves garlic, minced
1/2 tablespoon extra virgin olive oil
1/4 teaspoon ground coriander seeds
1/4 teaspoon crushed dried marjoram
Pinch black pepper
1 pound firm tofu
2–4 tablespoons canola oil

In a small bowl, combine all ingredients except tofu and canola oil and mix well. Cut the tofu into six 1/2-inch-thick slices and press to extract excess moisture. Place the tofu in a single layer in a shallow baking dish and pour marinade on top. Marinate at room temperature for 1 hour, turning tofu slices once.

In each of two skillets, heat 1–2 tablespoons of the canola oil over medium-low heat. Remove tofu from marinade. (Store marinade in a covered jar in the refrigerator and use again. It can be stored for up to 3 weeks.) Sauté the slices until lightly browned, 2–3 minutes; flip and brown the other side. Serve hot.

VARIATION: To broil the tofu slices, preheat broiler, arrange tofu in a single layer on an oiled baking sheet; brown top, turn, and brown the other side. Be careful not to overcook, or tofu will become dry and chewy.

Spinach Bombay with Tofu Cheese

Using tofu in place of cheese cuts the cholesterol out of this Indian-spiced dish. Serve it with Blood Orange and Lemon Salad (page 144) or any other dish that's rich in vitamin C. This will help your body convert the iron in the spinach to a form your body can more easily absorb.

2 teaspoons sesame oil
8 ounces firm tofu, cut into
   1/2-inch cubes
4 cloves garlic, minced
1/2 teaspoon turmeric
1/2 teaspoon sea salt

1/4 teaspoon chili powder
1/2 teaspoon Ginger Juice (page 241)
2 (10-ounce) packages fresh spinach,
   stemmed, washed and well-dried
1 tablespoon tahini
1 tablespoon fresh lemon juice

In a skillet, heat the oil over medium heat and sauté the tofu in 1 layer, turning until browned on each side, about 6 minutes. Add the garlic, turmeric, salt, chili powder, and ginger juice, and stir. Cook 2 minutes, then add the spinach and stir. Cover and let simmer for 3 minutes.

In a small bowl, mix together the tahini and lemon juice, and add to the tofu and spinach. Simmer until most of the liquid has cooked away, about 1 minute more.

Chinese Firecrackers

Cayenne pepper supplies the heat in this sweet and sour sauté. We've kept it on the mild side, so double up on the hot stuff if you want it to have more sizzle. Chili peppers, including cayenne, stimulate digestion. They also have a cooling effect on the body by helping to get heat to the surface where it can dissipate. Apple Berry Gel (page 234) makes a nice dessert after this dish.

2 cups canola or peanut oil for deep-frying
1 pound tofu, pressed briefly, and cut into $1/2$-inch cubes
3 tablespoons natural soy sauce
2 tablespoons rice syrup
1 tablespoon brown rice vinegar

$1/16$ teaspoon cayenne pepper
1 heaping tablespoon kuzu *dissolved in* 2 tablespoons cold water
1 scallion, sliced thin on the diagonal, for garnish

In a medium skillet, heat the oil and deep-fry the tofu cubes a few at a time. Each batch will take about 10 minutes. Drain fried tofu on paper towels.

In a small saucepan, mix the soy sauce, syrup, vinegar, cayenne pepper, and *kuzu* mixture, stirring until the *kuzu* is blended into the sauce. Bring to a boil, stirring often, until a thick sauce forms, about 5 minutes. Add the tofu to the sauce to heat through. Serve garnished with scallions.

Bok Choy, Shiitake Mushroom, and Tofu Stir-Fry

This dish is a study in contrasts of textures and flavors, in the true tradition of Chinese cooking. It sets mild, custard-soft tofu against crunchy bok choy and carrots, and chewy shiitake mushrooms. The roasted sesame oil and ginger lift the flavors of the other ingredients while the shiitakes add an earthy taste. Serve with brown rice or over cooked millet.

6–7 *dried shiitake mushrooms*
1 *medium bunch bok choy, or*
    3–4 bunches baby bok choy
1 *pound soft tofu, cut into ½-inch*
    cubes

3 *tablespoons natural soy sauce*
1 *tablespoon canola oil*
1–2 *tablespoons minced ginger*
2 *carrots, peeled and julienned*
1 *teaspoon dark sesame oil*

Bring 2 cups of water to a boil. Place the mushrooms in a bowl and add boiling water to cover. Soak for 20–30 minutes, until soft. Squeeze excess liquid from mushrooms. Remove and trim the stems, reserving them for another use. Quarter the caps or slice them into ¼-inch strips.

Meanwhile, wash the bok choy by separating the stalks and leaves. Cut stems from the leaves. Cut stems into 1-inch squares and leaves into strips.

Put the tofu into a bowl and sprinkle with 1 tablespoon of the soy sauce.

About 10 minutes before serving, heat a wok or large skillet. Add the canola oil, swirling to coat the sides of the wok or skillet. Add the ginger and stir-fry 15 seconds. Add the mushrooms and stir-fry over high heat 1 minute. Add the carrots and tofu and continue cooking over high heat 2 minutes. Add the bok choy stems and cook 30 seconds. Add the leaves and cook 2 minutes more. Cover occasionally to develop a bit of steam, and add a small amount of water if necessary to avoid sticking.

Season to taste with the remaining soy sauce and the dark sesame oil. Serve immediately.

5. *Vegetables*

America is the land of meat and potatoes, the place where vegetables are a food group many people love to hate. This is ironic, considering the virtues and variety vegetables can bring to our daily diet. They are a gold mine of nutrients, supplying nearly all the vitamins and minerals required for good health. Many of them also provide complex carbohydrates, dietary fiber, and even significant amounts of protein. Most important, vegetables supply their nutrients while remaining low in fat and calories. As if this were not enough, vegetables are an appealing way to bring color and variety to a meal: just think of baby carrots glazed with orange juice, a simple sauté of red and green peppers with red onions, or steaming fresh corn on the cob.

In 1992, the National Cancer Institute began promoting "5 a Day for Better Health" as a way of getting Americans to eat five servings a day of fruits and vegetables. For optimal health, though, the U.S. Department of Agriculture, in its Food Guide Pyramid, wants us to consume three to five servings a day of vegetables, plus two to four servings of fruits.

We realize most Americans rarely get past potatoes, tomatoes, and salad greens when they think about this food group. To gain all the benefits vegetables have to offer, you need to select regularly from all of the five basic types, namely: leafy (lettuce, kale, spinach); flower and stalks (broccoli, artichokes, asparagus); seeds and pods (peas, sweet corn, lima beans); roots and bulbs (carrots, potatoes, onions); and fruit vegetables (peppers, eggplant, squashes). Each group has its own nutritional advantages.

Green leafy vegetables are excellent sources of vitamin C and beta carotene, which is actually a precursor of vitamin A. According to the National Cancer Institute, beta carotene ranks high as a cancer-fighting food. Studies show that it can inhibit cancer of the skin, larynx, and lung. Consuming beta carotene is the preferred way to help the body get the important benefits of vitamin A, which is also available pre-formed from some vegetable and animal foods, especially fish oils and liver. At higher doses, this vitamin A can be toxic. However, beta carotene, which the body is able to convert into the vitamin A it needs, has little toxic potential, and it is, apparently, impossible to overdose on beta carotene. Leafy greens are also sources of chlorophyll, another substance being studied for its cancer-fighting properties. To date, it appears that people who consume significant amounts of dark green vegetables show a decreased risk of cancer of the prostate, lung, stomach, bladder, colon, and cervix. In addition, some greens—including members of the cruciferous (cabbage) family, like kale and mustard greens—contain sulforaphane, a chemical that stimulates protective enzymes known to inhibit the growth of tumors.

Flower and stalk vegetables tend to be rich in vitamin C, calcium, potassium, and dietary fiber. Although some, like celery, are not particularly rich in nutrients, others, like broccoli and cauliflower, are nutrient powerhouses, containing good amounts of beta carotene and vitamin C.

Seed and pod vegetables contain the parts of the plant that store energy. They provide more protein and carbohydrates than other vegetables and are rich in B vitamins, zinc, potassium, iron, and calcium. A cup of fresh peas, for example, contains as much protein as a large egg, without the saturated fat or cholesterol. And peas are high in soluble fiber, which helps lower cholesterol, and potassium, which helps control blood pressure. Plus, they contribute thiamine, an important anti-stress nutrient. Taken all together, these nutrients make peas a remarkable, heart-healthy food.

Root vegetables are underground nutrient storehouses. Starchy and dense, they can be the most satisfying vegetable foods. They offer other advantages as well. Potatoes, for example, are surprisingly good sources of vitamin C. Just half a baked potato supplies nearly 25 percent of the RDA. Sweet potatoes and carrots contain abundant beta carotene; radishes and turnips contribute soluble fiber and vitamin C; and bulbs like onions and garlic contain sulfur compounds that help lower blood pressure and cholesterol levels.

Certain fruits that we categorize as vegetables, including peppers, tomatoes, and squashes, are often the highest sources of both vitamin C and beta-carotene. By weight, green bell peppers contain twice as much vitamin C as citrus fruits, red bell peppers three times as much, and chili peppers even more. Chili peppers offer another nutritional benefit: capsaicin, the chemical responsible for their heat, acts in the human body as an anticoagulant and blood thinner that can help prevent heart attacks or strokes caused by blood clots.

Crucifers show the most health-promoting promise of all the vegetable groups. Known for their cross-shaped flowers (hence their name), cruciferous vegetables include cabbages, broccoli, brussels sprouts, cauliflower, kale, collards, and mustard greens, as well as such root vegetables as rutabagas and turnips. Every one of these contains cancer-fighting nitrogen compounds called indoles, which protect against cancer of the stomach and large intestine. They also contain other compounds that stimulate our bodies to release cancer-fighting enzymes. Plus, they are an excellent source of antioxidant nutrients like beta carotene and vitamin C, which block cancer-promoting oxygen molecules known as free radicals. Some, especially greens like kale, collards, and turnip greens, are also leading vegetable sources of calcium. Many of the *Natural Health* recipes focus on using one or more of the health-promoting cruciferous vegetables.

These recipes prove how delicious as well as nutritious vegetables can be. They even show how to enjoy vegetables in the center of your plate—not just on the side.

Leeks Vinaigrette

Leeks have a milder and sweeter flavor than onions and stay slightly crunchy when cooked. Commonly added to soups and stews, they are delicious when served on their own. Leeks supply more vitamins and minerals than scallions and are a moderate source of iron, folic acid, and vitamins B_6 and C.

8 slender leeks
　Pinch sea salt
3 tablespoons extra virgin olive oil

1 tablespoon fresh lemon juice
$^1/_4$ teaspoon dried tarragon

Cut the leeks lengthwise down the center, leaving the root end intact so the leaves can be spread for washing thoroughly under cold running water. Cut off the tougher green tops, saving the lighter green leaves from the center for stock and discarding the tough, dark outer leaves.

Place the leeks in one layer in a large shallow pan and almost cover with water. Add the salt and bring to a boil. Reduce the heat and simmer, covered, 7 minutes. Uncover and continue to simmer until nearly all the water has cooked away. Immediately transfer the cooked leeks to a serving dish.

In a small bowl, mix together the oil, lemon juice, and tarragon, and pour over the leeks while they are hot. Chill in the refrigerator 4 hours, or overnight, before serving.

Asparagus with Ginger Citrus Dressing

Snapping off the tough bottom ends of asparagus with your fingers is a sure way to eliminate what you don't want while keeping every deliciously edible inch. Asparagus is rich in three nutrients that can help protect us against cancer—beta carotene, vitamin C, and selenium. Serve this dish as a first course or as a vegetable side dish.

$^{1}/_{2}$-inch-piece ginger
1 orange
1 tablespoon extra virgin olive oil
2 teaspoons balsamic vinegar

$^{1}/_{4}$ teaspoon sea salt
$^{1}/_{4}$ teaspoon freshly ground pepper
$^{1}/_{4}$ teaspoon natural soy sauce
1 pound asparagus (about 24 stalks)

Peel the ginger and cut into matchsticks. Wash the orange well. With a sharp paring knife, cut off strips of zest from half the orange, and julienne the strips.

In a small saucepan, boil the ginger and zest in $1^{1}/_{2}$ cups cold water to remove any bitterness, about 5 minutes. Drain.

Juice the orange and put $^{1}/_{4}$ cup of the juice in a small bowl. Reserve remaining juice for some other use. Whisk the olive oil, vinegar, salt, pepper, and soy sauce into the orange juice mixture. Stir in the ginger and zest. Let sit an hour for best flavor.

Snap off the tough ends of the asparagus. In a steamer basket in a large pot, steam until the stalks turn bright green and are tender but not soft, about 6 minutes. Put the hot asparagus on a platter, pour the dressing over, and serve.

Zucchini with Fresh Mint

This is wonderfully fresh-tasting summer side dish. Mint has a long history of use in folk medicine as a tonic, digestive aid, and reliever of nervous tension. Also, it is often used to make tea. Here, you can enjoy its benefits with the fresh, whole mint leaves. Serve with Grilled Salmon Steaks with Red Onion (page 137).

4–6 *small zucchini*
8–10 *mint leaves, torn into small pieces*
2 *cloves garlic, minced*

1/4 *cup brown rice vinegar*
2 *tablespoons extra virgin olive oil*
1/4 *teaspoon sea salt*

Slice the zucchini lengthwise into thin pieces. In a steamer basket in a large pot, steam the zucchini until tender, about 5 minutes. Remove and, while hot, mix in a serving bowl with the mint leaves, garlic, vinegar, oil, and salt. Serve immediately.

Lemon Cinnamon Beets

If you think you don't like beets, try them prepared this way. The lemon juice actually brings out the natural sweetness of the beets while adding a slight edge of acidity. A serving of beets is a good way to help fill your daily requirements for beta carotene, calcium, and iron. Serve with Quinoa Timbales with Pine Nuts (page 47).

4–5 *medium beets (about 2 pounds)*
  2 *tablespoons apple juice*
  $1/2$ *teaspoon sea salt*
  $1/4$ *teaspoon cinnamon*
  Juice of $1/2$ lemon

1 *tablespoon* kuzu *diluted in*
  2 tablespoons cold water
  Parsley sprigs and lemon wedges, for garnish

Scrub the beets and place them in a medium pot. Cover with water and boil until tender, about 45 minutes. Drain, reserving 1 cup of the cooking water. As soon as the beets are cool enough to handle, rub away the skins, and slice the beets into thin rounds.

In a medium saucepan, combine the beets with the reserved beet water, apple juice, salt, cinnamon, and lemon juice. Mix in the *kuzu* and simmer until mixture thickens. Garnish with parsley sprigs and lemon wedges.

Maque Choux

Legend has it that the Choctaw Indians gave the corn stew known as *maque choux* to the Cajuns. This colorful version combines green bell pepper, red tomato, and yellow corn. Serve this dish together with Red Beans and Rice (page 121) or a dairy dish. The amino acids in either will complement those in the corn and produce a complete protein.

  2 tablespoons corn oil
1½ cups diced onion (1–2 medium
    onions)
  1 cup diced green bell pepper
1¼ cups seeded and diced ripe tomatoes
    (about 3 medium tomatoes)

  4 cups fresh or frozen corn kernels
    (4 large ears)
½ teaspoon sea salt
¼ teaspoon black pepper

In a large heavy pan, heat the oil. Add the onion, pepper, and tomatoes. Sauté until partially softened, 3–4 minutes. Add the corn, and season with salt and pepper. Cover and simmer until the corn is lightly cooked, 8–10 minutes.

Roasted Peppers with Anchovies

Sweet peppers and anchovies are a typical antipasto on the Italian table. Anchovies are salty but very nutritious: they are rich in the essential omega-3 fatty acids that are difficult to obtain from vegetable foods. Omega-3 fatty acids help lower blood cholesterol. Here, the anchovies serve as a hearty seasoning for the peppers. Serve the peppers on toasted Italian bread or accompanying grilled tuna fish.

4 *green bell peppers*
1 *red bell pepper*
1 *(2-ounce) can anchovies, drained*

10 *cloves garlic, peeled and steamed until*
   soft, about 10 minutes
2 *tablespoons extra virgin olive oil*

Preheat oven to 350 degrees.

Place the whole peppers on a baking sheet and bake until soft and browned, about 20 minutes, turning peppers every 5 minutes for even cooking. Remove from oven and place in a paper bag for 10 minutes to allow steam to soften the skins. Peel the peppers, cut them open, and discard the seeds. Cut the peppers into strips.

Chop the anchovies. Place the garlic, anchovies, and oil in a small mixing bowl and mash until a paste is formed.

In a mixing bowl, toss the peppers with anchovy-garlic paste. Let sit at least 15 minutes before using.

Quick Curried Vegetables

If you have run out of ideas for serving vegetables, try this low-fat curry. The seasonings heighten the flavor of any sautéed autumn vegetable; add some chopped apple or vary the combination of vegetables if you like. Our favorite blends include tomatoes, green beans, and onions, or zucchini, eggplant, and sweet peppers. Serve with Shrimp Biryani (page 133).

1 teaspoon sesame oil
1/8 teaspoon cinnamon
1/2 teaspoon curry powder
1/4 teaspoon turmeric
1/4 teaspoon ground cumin

1/4 teaspoon ground coriander
1/4 teaspoon sea salt
3 cups diced mixed vegetables (carrots, turnips, acorn, or other hard winter squash, green cabbage)

In a medium pot, heat the oil. Add the cinnamon, curry powder, turmeric, cumin, coriander, and salt. Stir to blend. Add the vegetables and sauté briefly. Add ½ cup of water, cover, and simmer until vegetables are cooked.

Parsnips in Sweet Miso

Parsnips are traditionally served buttered, fried, or made into fritters. Parsnips are also delicious cooked without all that fat; the mildly sweet-salty flavor of a simple sweet miso sauce is perfect with the natural sweetness of the parsnips. Serve this hearty winter dish with Gingered Tempeh with Basil (page 82).

4 large parsnips, peeled and cut into
bite-size pieces

2 tablespoons sweet miso

Place the parsnips in a medium pan with a tight-fitting lid. Dilute the miso in ¼ cup of water and add to the parsnips. Cover, bring to a simmer, and simmer until parsnips are cooked, about 25 minutes, stirring gently about halfway through. Remove the lid and bring to a boil, allowing most of the liquid to evaporate. Serve immediately.

Glazed Carrots and Snow Peas

It is best to eat carrots fresh, since canned carrots lose half their vitamin C and beta carotene, but using raw carrots can get monotonous. In this bright variation on carrots and peas, *mirin* and *kuzu* make a sauce that plays up the natural sweetness of both vegetables. Serve with any broiled fish or with Black Pepper Tofu Steaks (page 83).

2 *large carrots*
2 *teaspoons sesame oil*
1 *teaspoon peeled and minced ginger*
¹/₄ *teaspoon sea salt*

¹/₄ *pound snow peas*
2 *tablespoons* mirin
2 *teaspoons* kuzu *dissolved in*
   1 tablespoon water

Cut the carrots on the diagonal into ¹/₈-inch-thick slices, then cut each slice lengthwise into two or three pieces.

In a medium skillet, heat the oil. Add the carrots, ginger, and salt. Sauté briefly, just until the carrots turn a brighter color. Add ¹/₄ cup water, cover, and cook until the carrots are tender-crisp, about 5 minutes. Add the snow peas, toss, cover, and cook for 30 seconds. Uncover and remove from heat. If any liquid remains in the pan, pour it off, retaining ¹/₃ cup. Add the *mirin* to this water.

Add the *kuzu* to the *mirin* mixture. Pour over the vegetables. Bring to a boil over medium heat, stirring constantly until the sauce thickens and becomes translucent. Simmer for 1 minute, and serve immediately.

Cauliflower with Black Pepper and Orange Allioli

SERVES 6–8

In Catalonia, a part of Spain, garlicky allioli is used as frequently as we use ketchup. Catalonians might present this dish as part of *tapas,* a kind of small snack; we like it as a side dish or served as part of an antipasto. Cauliflower is surprisingly high in vitamin C and potassium. A touch of fresh cilantro (a member of the carrot family) adds vitamin A as well as iron and phosphorus to this zesty dish. Serve with Corn Bread Baked Beans (page 122) or as a salad accompanying grilled fish.

¹/₂ teaspoon sea salt
1 strip lemon zest
1 head cauliflower, broken into florets

¹/₃ cup Black Pepper and Orange Allioli
(recipe follows)
Chopped fresh cilantro, for garnish

In a large pot, bring 6 cups of water to a boil with the salt and lemon zest. Add the cauliflower and boil until it is just tender, 4–5 minutes. Drain and rinse under cold water to stop the cooking. Toss with the Black Pepper and Orange Allioli and garnish with cilantro.

(continued on next page)

Black Pepper and Orange Allioli

MAKES ⅔ CUP

Serve this pungent, mayonnaiselike sauce on other steamed vegetables and with grilled fish. Using a mortar and pestle gives this sauce its creamy texture. If you do not have a mortar and pestle, make the allioli in a blender.

3 cloves garlic, minced
½ teaspoon sea salt
½ cup extra virgin olive oil

2 tablespoons orange juice
1 tablespoon grated orange zest
¼ teaspoon black pepper

Place the garlic and salt in a mortar and with a pestle gently mash to a thick paste. Add the oil a little at a time, stirring well after each addition. Whisk in orange juice, zest, and pepper until creamy. If using a blender, puree the garlic with the salt. With the blender running, drizzle in the oil, followed by the orange juice. Scrape the sauce out of the blender and mix in the orange zest and pepper.

Sweet Potato Croquettes

This unusual dish comes out crisp on the outside and creamy on the inside. Sweet potatoes are a good source of vitamins A and C and the pine nuts add thiamine, iron, and magnesium. Serve as a side dish, or double up portions and let these sweet potato balls be the main course.

2 cups baked or boiled sweet potatoes,
    mashed (1–2 medium potatoes)
^{1}/$_4$ teaspoon sea salt
^{1}/$_4$ teaspoon mace
^{1}/$_4$ teaspoon freshly ground nutmeg

3 tablespoons canola oil
^{1}/$_4$ cup finely chopped pine nuts
1 cup dry whole-wheat bread crumbs
    Peanut oil for frying

In a bowl, combine the potatoes, salt, mace, nutmeg, and oil. Chill well.

In a bowl, crush together nuts and bread crumbs to form a fine crumb. Roll the potato mixture into 1-inch balls, and roll in the nut and bread crumb mixture. In a skillet over medium-high heat, heat the peanut oil. Fry the breaded potato balls until browned and crisp on the outside and heated inside, about 5 minutes. Drain on paper towels and serve immediately.

Stuffed Spanish Onions

In Italy, onions stuffed with ground meat or seasoned bread crumbs are often part of the antipasto table. Here, they are given a decidedly American twist. The colorful filling is well-spiced and full of vitamin C, while corn adds protein. Serve this dish as a vegetable or at the center of the plate, accompanied by Mediterranean Bean Salad (page 124).

4 large Spanish onions (about 3 pounds)
3 teaspoons natural soy sauce
1 tablespoon olive oil
4 cloves garlic, minced
1 teaspoon sea salt
1/2 teaspoon dried red pepper flakes
1 tablespoon ground cumin

1 teaspoon ground coriander
1 cup diced red bell pepper
1/2 cup diced green bell pepper
1 cup fresh or frozen corn kernels
   (1 large ear)
4 tablespoons bread crumbs
4 sprigs cilantro

Preheat oven to 350 degrees. Peel onions and trim off the root ends, so that each onion sits squarely on a flat surface. Cut off the top, shoot end so that you can pick out the middle of each onion, leaving the two or three outermost layers intact. Sprinkle 1/2 teaspoon of the soy sauce into each onion. Dice enough of the scooped-out onion to yield 1/2 cup.

In a skillet over high heat, heat the oil and brown the diced onion and the garlic with the salt, 2–3 minutes. Add the chili pepper, cumin, and coriander, and stir. Add the red and green peppers and the corn, reduce heat to medium, and sauté until tender. If necessary, add a little water to keep the spices from burning.

Remove from heat, and stir in the bread crumbs. Fill the onions with the mixture.

Pour a little water and the remaining soy sauce into a baking dish just large enough to hold the onions. Sit the onions in the dish. Cover with foil and bake until you can easily pierce the onions with a toothpick, about 45 minutes. The onions should still be firm enough to hold their shape. Garnish each onion with a sprig of cilantro. Serve hot or at room temperature.

Glazed Acorn Squash

Unlike most winter squashes, acorns are not a good source of beta carotene, but they *are* rich in calcium. A cup of baked acorn squash provides 90 milligrams of calcium (about 11 percent of the RDA) and only 100 calories. This is a festive side dish spiced with cloves and cinnamon and glazed with its own juices. It goes well with Sweet and Sour Red Cabbage with Seitan (page 76).

1 small acorn squash
¼ cup mirin
½ cinnamon stick

4 whole cloves
¼ teaspoon sea salt

Preheat oven to 300 degrees. Warm a baking dish large enough to hold the squash.

Quarter, seed, and peel the squash. Cut crosswise into ½-inch-thick slices. In a medium saucepan, combine the squash with the *mirin,* cinnamon stick, cloves, and sea salt, and add ½ cup water. Bring to a boil, cover, and reduce heat to a simmer. Cook until the squash is tender, 15–20 minutes. With a slotted spoon, immediately transfer the squash to the heated dish, reserving the cooking liquid. Cover dish with foil and place in oven.

Strain the cooking liquid, return it to saucepan, and cook down, uncovered, to half the volume, about 3 tablespoons, taking care to avoid burning the glaze. Pour glaze over squash and serve.

Ital Run Down

In Jamaica, coconut prepared in this way is called *Run Down.* It's a great way to spark up vegetables; use any combination you like. Although coconut is high in saturated fat, this dish is a wonderful treat to enjoy from time to time.

2 cups Unsweetened Coconut Milk
  (page 242)
8 scallions
2 cups carrots cut in (^{1}/$_2$-inch chunks,
  about ^{2}/$_3$ pound)

2 cups peeled, seeded, and cut butternut
  squash (in 1-inch chunks)
^{1}/$_2$ cup chopped celery (about 1 stalk)
2 teaspoons dried thyme
^{1}/$_8$ teaspoon black pepper

In a large skillet, bring the coconut milk to a rapid boil and cook until it begins to thicken, about 5 minutes. Skim off the oil. Add the other ingredients, cover, and simmer until the vegetables are tender, about 20 minutes. Add water as necessary to make the sauce the consistency of custard.

Dark Greens with Oregano and Wakame

Mustard greens resemble kale, but they have a stronger bite. Ounce for ounce, mustard greens have as much calcium as whole milk. By cooking the greens with *wakame,* a leafy sea vegetable with a mild, fresh flavor, this dish becomes a rich source of essential trace minerals. Serve with Sweet Potato Croquettes (page 101).

1 *bunch mustard greens, about*
   1½ pounds
1 *tablespoon extra virgin olive oil*
1½ *cups sliced onion (sliced in half moons,*
   1–2 medium onions)
2 *cloves garlic, minced*

½ *teaspoon dried oregano*
2 *(5-inch) strips* wakame, *soaked for*
   10 minutes and cut into 1-inch pieces
½ *tablespoon* kuzu *dissolved in ¼ cup*
   water
2 *tablespoons natural soy sauce*

In a large pot, steam greens until just tender, about 5 minutes. Cool and cut into 2-inch pieces. (There should be about 6 cups.)

In a large skillet, heat the oil. Sauté the onion and garlic until the onions are tender, 3–5 minutes. Sprinkle the oregano over the mixture. Add the mustard greens and *wakame,* and sauté until greens are wilted, about 3 minutes. Add the *kuzu* mixture and soy sauce. Cook, stirring constantly, until the sauce thickens. Turn off heat and let sit 15 minutes before serving.

Cajun Kale Salad

If you don't like kale, this colorful dish could change your mind. The corn and spicy seasoning go perfectly with the crunchy texture of the greens. Reusing the cooking water from the corn for cooking the kale gives the greens delicious sweetness. Kale is a cruciferous vegetable and a nutritional powerhouse, rich in vitamin C, beta carotene, and fiber. It's a good source of calcium and iron, as well. Serve this salad with Louisiana Shrimp Stew (page 139).

4 ears sweet corn
1 small bunch kale, about 1 pound
1 large red bell pepper, diced
1 green bell pepper, diced
1 small Vidalia onion or red onion, minced

1 small clove garlic, minced
1–1½ teaspoons Cajun Spice Mix (recipe follows)
2 tablespoons fresh lemon juice
2 tablespoons extra virgin olive oil

In a large pot, bring 2 cups of water to a boil and add the corn. Cook until bright yellow, about 5 minutes. Remove with tongs and reserve 1 cup of the cooking water. Cool the corn and cut kernels from cobs. Place the kernels in a large mixing bowl.

Wash the kale in a large basin of cold water. Strip the leaves from the tough stems and discard stems. Chop the leaves medium-fine. Bring the reserved cooking water to a boil, add the kale, and cook until just tender and still bright green, about 5 minutes. Remove from the liquid with a slotted spoon and spread on a large plate to cool quickly.

When the kale is cool, squeeze to extract as much water as possible. Toss the kale with the cooked corn kernels, peppers, onion, garlic, and cajun spice mix. Just before serving, toss with the lemon juice, and olive oil.

Cajun Spice Mix

2 teaspoons paprika
$^{1}/_{2}$ teaspoon cayenne pepper
$^{1}/_{4}$ teaspoon freshly ground black pepper

$^{1}/_{4}$ teaspoon ground allspice
$^{1}/_{2}$ teaspoon dried thyme
$^{1}/_{4}$ teaspoon freshly ground white pepper

In a small bowl, mix all ingredients thoroughly. Store the mixture in an airtight container.

Spring Greens with Pine Nuts

SERVES 4

The young leafy tops of turnips are one of the sharpest-tasting spring greens. They are also one of the greens highest in vitamin C and calcium. The simple dressing of this dish complements the greens' bitter flavor, and the pine nuts create a contrast of color and texture while supplying extra iron and protein.

1 large bunch turnip greens, about
   2 pounds
1 tablespoon pine nuts
2 teaspoons dark sesame oil

1 tablespoon brown rice vinegar
1 tablespoon plus 1 teaspoon natural soy
   sauce

Wash the greens, and remove tough stems from leaves. In a large pot, steam greens until just tender or color changes to bright green, about 5 minutes. Remove and toss gently to cool.

In a dry small skillet over medium heat, toast the pine nuts, stirring constantly, until they are lightly browned and fragrant. Reserve a few nuts for garnish and combine the rest with the greens. In individual serving bowls, arrange the greens in small pyramids. Sprinkle the reserved pine nuts over the greens.

In a small bowl, combine the oil, vinegar, and soy sauce, and mix well. Pour about 2 teaspoons over each pyramid of greens just before serving.

Grilled Radicchio

Deep red radicchio is a member of the chicory family. Italians often serve this bitter vegetable grilled. If you don't have an outdoor grill, the broiler works quite nicely. Just be sure to set the rack in the position farthest from the heat source. Serve with Steamed Salmon Piccante (page 131).

4 whole small heads radicchio (about 1½ pounds)

¼ cup extra virgin olive oil
Sea salt

Cut each head of radicchio lengthwise into eight wedges. Brush each wedge generously with the olive oil, and season with salt. Place wedges on a grill over low coals and cook, turning frequently, until the outer leaves are barely wilted and some edges are lightly charred, about 5 minutes. If you like, drizzle with more of a fruity extra virgin olive oil before serving.

Steamed Broccoli with Walnut Miso

SERVES 4–6

Broccoli is one of the most healthful foods you can eat. A cruciferous vegetable, it contains special nitrogen compounds called *indoles,* which are effective in preventing certain forms of cancer. In addition, broccoli is a rich source of vitamin C and beta carotene. The walnut and miso make a rich, savory seasoning for the broccoli. Serve with Cod Fillets en Papillote (page 129), grilled eggplant slices, or over pasta.

1 bunch broccoli, about 1½ pounds
¼ cup walnuts

1 tablespoon red miso

Cut the tops of the broccoli into florets. Peel the tough skin from the stems and slice the tender parts into bite-size pieces, keeping the florets and stems separate. Pour an inch of water into a large pot. Add the sliced broccoli stems, cover, and bring just to a boil. Add the florets. Cook over high heat until florets are tender but still bright green, about 3 minutes. Drain the broccoli, reserving ½ cup of the cooking water. Put broccoli in a bowl and cover to keep it warm.

In a heavy dry skillet, toast the walnuts until fragrant, 5–8 minutes, stirring constantly to prevent burning. In a mortar or food processor, grind the nuts to a paste. Add the miso. Gradually add the cooking water by the spoonful until you have a thick paste. Toss the warm broccoli with the walnut-miso paste. Serve immediately.

Irish Chestnuts and Brussels Sprouts

Brussels sprouts and chestnuts are a traditional combination in Ireland and England. Brussels sprouts, a member of the cabbage family, contain the same cancer-fighting properties. Sweet chestnuts are a delicious, low-fat source of protein. Use fresh or frozen chestnuts for this warming winter recipe. Serve with French-style Braised Tempeh (page 78).

2 cups fresh chestnuts
2 cups brussels sprouts

Pinch sea salt

Preheat oven to 400 degrees. With a sharp knife, slit the chestnuts, making a cross at the narrow end. Place them in the oven for 10–15 minutes. Peel while still hot, removing both outer shell and inner skins, taking care not to break the nuts.

Remove the outer leaves of the sprouts, and trim their bases. Cut a cross on the bottom of each sprout so it will cook evenly. In a large, shallow pan, bring ¼ cup of water and the salt to a boil. Add the sprouts and simmer, covered, 10 minutes. Add the chestnuts and simmer until all the water is evaporated and the sprouts are still bright green, about 5 minutes longer. Toss lightly and serve.

VARIATION: Cut carrots into bite-size pieces and use instead of brussels sprouts, giving the carrots an extra 10 minutes of cooking time before adding the chestnuts.

6. Beans

Beans and other legumes, including peas, lentils, and soybeans, supply more protein than any other vegetable source. The diet of most people around the world consists mainly of beans eaten with a grain. While the protein in both legumes and grains is incomplete, being deficient in one or more of the essential amino acids, pairing the two foods provides high-quality protein equal to that of meat and other animal sources. Protein from beans has the advantage of containing little of the saturated fat and none of the cholesterol that protein from animal sources provides. So while a 100-gram serving of cooked kidney beans supplies 9 grams of protein, no cholesterol, and almost no fat, the same size serving of sirloin steak provides 30 grams of protein, but also 9 grams of fat—30 percent of which is saturated—and 90 milligrams of cholesterol.

Legumes also provide soluble fiber. Only wheat bran is a better dietary source of fiber than beans, which supply 9 grams per cooked cup. Researchers have found that eating a cup of cooked beans each day can significantly reduce both harmful LDL cholesterol and blood pressure. The soluble fiber in beans also helps increase stool bulk, which alleviates some digestive disorders and may also help prevent colon cancer.

Like grains, beans contain protease inhibitors, enzymes that help fight cancer at the cellular level. Plus, beans are excellent sources of iron. Although the iron in beans (and all vegetable foods) is nonheme iron, which the body does not absorb as well as the iron in animal foods, eating beans along with foods rich in vitamin C, like tomatoes and peppers, dramatically increases the amount of iron absorbed. Our Sweet Pepper Pinto Bean Chili (page 120) is a good example, with red bell peppers, tomatoes, and chili powder providing the vitamin C our bodies need to get the most iron out of this dish. Based on research in Asia, scientists here are beginning to study whether soybeans and lentils—which may contain a precursor of estrogen known as protoestrogen—benefit menopausal women.

People often avoid eating beans for two reasons. The first is that they find legumes cause gas and bloating. The second is the long cooking time required to prepare beans. There are simple ways to avoid both these problems.

Beans do contain certain indigestible complex sugars. When they pass undigested into the intestines, these sugars ferment into gas. The easiest way to reduce the gas-producing properties of beans is to soak them in water, discard the soaking water, and cook the beans in completely fresh water. Some people also claim that adding a piece of *kombu,* a kind of kelp, to the pot while cooking beans helps reduce flatulence. This sea vegetable adds flavor, so we suggest trying it to see what effects this method has for you. Discard the *kombu* once the beans are cooked.

Eating beans early in the day, instead of later, when the digestive system is less active, also may help you digest them more comfortably. At any time, it is better to eat beans in several ½-cup quantities than to eat a large amount at once.

Dried beans do not have to take all day to cook. Soaking them for eight to twelve hours before cooking will help; four hours may be sufficient for smaller beans. You can also hasten the soaking process by bringing a cup of dried beans to a boil in three cups of water in a covered pot. As soon as the pot boils, turn off the heat. Let the covered pot sit for one hour, drain the beans, then add fresh water and cook as you would normally.

Adding salt or acidic foods such as tomatoes and vinegar to beans hardens their skins, so add these ingredients only when your beans are almost completely done. There is one exception: lima beans tend to crumble easily; adding salt while they cook helps prevent this. Lastly, buy dried beans that have been harvested within the past year. They will cook more quickly and have fuller flavor than beans that have been sitting around for ages.

Canned beans can be used in place of cooked or dried ones in many recipes.

When buying canned beans, read the label to be sure they do not contain sugar or additives such as sulfites. This will not be a problem if you buy canned organic beans, which can be found at natural food stores and some supermarkets. Rinse canned beans before using them to remove excess sodium.

Dried beans sold in supermarkets include:

BLACK *(Turtle Beans)*—Used in Mexican dishes and Southern black-bean soup. Also good for making vegetarian chili.

BLACK-EYED PEAS—Popular in the South and Texas, where they are used to make Hoppin' John. They have a distinctive flavor and soft texture. Black-eyed peas can be found frozen and fresh as well as dried and in cans.

CHICK-PEAS *(Garbanzo Beans)*—A staple of Mediterranean cooking. In the Middle East chick-peas are used in *hummus,* a spread made with tahini. In southern France, they are used in *garbure,* a thick soup. Chick-peas are also dried and ground into flour that can be used to make fritters. Canned chick-peas often work well in place of dried, though they have a blander taste and a softer texture.

GREAT NORTHERN—A white bean used for making baked beans and French cassoulet, a stew made with pork and duck.

KIDNEY—May be red or white. The red are good for red rice and beans, salads, and chili. White kidney beans, also called *cannellini* beans, are good for making Mediterranean salads and minestrone.

LENTILS—A member of the pea family, they come in red, green, and brown varieties. Red lentils may cook in as little as twenty minutes; green French de Puy lentils require forty-five minutes to an hour. Good for soups, stews, chili, salads, Indian *dal,* and curries.

LIMA BEANS—Large dried limas make a sweet, creamy thick soup. Smaller lima beans are good cooked with dried mushrooms.

NAVY—The bean used in famous Senate bean soup (write your senator for the recipe). Also good in stews.

PINTO—The most popular bean for chili and Mexican refried beans. Also good in soups.

SPLIT PEAS *(Green and Yellow)*—These legumes do not require soaking. Used to make split-pea soup. Yellow peas can also be used to make *dal.*

Other Beans

A variety of other kinds of beans can be found at natural food stores, including *adzuki,* small red beans with a dry, pronounced flavor, which are good in stews, particularly with pumpkin and winter squashes; *mung beans,* small green beans, often used in Indian cooking, that may be cooked or sprouted; and *soybeans,* which take an exceptionally long time to cook—using a pressure cooker is recommended.

Specialty and natural food stores are beginning to carry a wider variety of colorful beans, including dappled brown-and-white *anasazi,* golden-brown dried *fava,* and mottled *Christmas lima beans.*

While dried beans keep without spoiling, they stay fresh longer when stored in a cool, dry, dark place. Plan to use dried beans within six months of the time you buy them. After that, they may not soften up enough when cooked to be enjoyable.

Kabuli Chole

This chick-pea stew is full of Indian flavors, from curry powder and *garam masala,* an Indian blend of spices. You can make *garam masala* or buy it at Indian and natural food stores. Make the *chole* a day or two ahead so the spices and seasonings have time to marry together. Serve with white or brown basmati rice.

2 tablespoons canola oil
1 cup thinly sliced onion (about
   1 medium onion)
1 tablespoon peeled and minced ginger
1 teaspoon coriander seeds
1 teaspoon cumin seeds
1 teaspoon black mustard seeds
1 teaspoon curry powder

1½ pounds fresh tomatoes, seeded and
   pureed
1 green bell pepper, diced
1 red bell pepper, diced
3 cups cooked chick-peas
3 tablespoons plain yogurt
1 tablespoon Garam Masala
   (page 240)

In a large, heavy skillet, heat the oil over medium-low heat. Add the onion, ginger, coriander, cumin, mustard, and curry powder. Sauté, stirring frequently, until the onion is tender, about 10 minutes. Add the tomatoes and simmer, uncovered, 10 minutes. Add the peppers and chick-peas, reduce heat, cover, and simmer 30 minutes, stirring occasionally. If the stew seems too thin, cook it uncovered to thicken.

To serve, stir in the yogurt and *garam masala.* Serve with *chapati,* a flat Indian bread, whole-wheat pita bread, or crackers.

Navy Beans with Garlic and Collard Greens

SERVES 4

Beans and greens are a natural pair, providing the double nutritional lift of vitamins A and C plus beta carotene. When you are pressed for time, canned cannellini beans can stand in for home-cooked navy beans. Serve with Tomatoes Stuffed with Savory Bread Crumbs (page 199).

1 tablespoon extra virgin olive oil
2 cloves garlic, minced
3 cups chopped collard greens, kale, or mustard greens

1 cup cooked navy beans
1 tablespoon natural soy sauce
    Dash black pepper

In a large skillet over medium-low heat, heat the oil. Add the garlic and sauté briefly, being careful not to let it brown. Add the greens and sauté until wilted, 1–2 minutes. Toss in the beans, soy sauce, and pepper, and sauté a minute more. Add water to barely cover the bottom of the pan, cover, and cook until greens are just tender.

Himalayan Lentils

When you want a solid meal and don't have time to spend standing over the stove, make lentils and a pot of rice. Onions sautéed with aromatic spices add Indian flavor to this dish. Leftovers make a delicious lentil salad when served at room temperature.

1 cup brown lentils
3-inch-strip kombu
2 bay leaves
1 tablespoon sesame oil
1 cup diced onion (about 1 medium onion)
3 cloves garlic, minced
¼ teaspoon ground turmeric
¼ teaspoon ground cumin

¼ teaspoon ground coriander
¼ teaspoon ground cinnamon
¼ teaspoon ground cardamom
½ teaspoon sea salt
2 teaspoons peeled and grated ginger
¼ teaspoon chili powder
Chopped fresh cilantro, parsley, or scallions, for garnish

Spread the lentils on a plate and check carefully for stones. Place the lentils in a pot and rinse in a few changes of water.

In a medium pot, combine the lentils and *kombu* with 4 cups of water. Bring to a boil, lower heat, and simmer 30 minutes. Add the bay leaves and more water if needed. Continue to simmer slowly until the lentils are tender.

Meanwhile, in a skillet, heat the oil, add the onion, and sauté. When the onion begins to brown, stir in the garlic, turmeric, cumin, coriander, cinnamon, and cardamom. Add the salt and ginger. Stir and sauté for 2 minutes, then add the mixture to the lentils. Add the chili powder. Let simmer, stirring occasionally and tasting to test for balance and flavor, about 20 minutes. Remove the bay leaves, garnish and serve.

Oriental Refried Beans

Instead of using lard, as in traditional Mexican cooking, we prepare these refried beans with olive oil. Miso and lemon juice add zing. If you want to add heat, stir in some diced canned chili peppers, hot sauce, or salsa. Serve as a side dish, or rolled inside tortillas or chapatis.

2 tablespoons extra virgin olive oil
1 cup diced onion (about 1 medium onion)
3 cloves garlic, minced
2 cups cooked pinto beans, cooking water reserved

$^1/_2$ teaspoon natural soy sauce
1 tablespoon rice miso
1 tablespoon fresh lemon juice

In a heavy skillet, heat the oil and sauté the onion and garlic until translucent, 5–10 minutes. Add the drained beans, and cook 2–3 minutes. Stir in $^1/_3$ cup of the bean cooking water and the soy sauce, and partially mash the beans with a fork.

In a small bowl, combine the miso and lemon juice, and mix into the beans. If the beans seem dry, add more of the bean cooking water. Cook 1 minute more.

Serve with a variety of toppings and garnishes, such as chopped scallions, sliced olives, grated carrots, shredded lettuce, and sprouts.

Vegetable Chick-pea Fritters with Ginger Dip

SERVES 4

Chick-pea flour, which can be found in natural food stores, or stores specializing in Indian and Middle Eastern foods, makes lighter, more protein-packed fritters than whole-wheat flour. Before using, toast the flour in a heavy dry skillet to bring out its flavor.

$2^1/_4$ cups coarsely grated yellow summer squash
$^1/_2$ cup diced green bell pepper
$^1/_4$ cup thinly sliced scallions
1 clove garlic, minced
3 tablespoons minced parsley
1 teaspoon sea salt
$^1/_4$ teaspoon white pepper

1 egg, beaten
1 cup toasted chick-pea flour
$^1/_4$ cup unbleached white flour
1 teaspoon nonaluminum baking powder
$^1/_2$ teaspoon dried basil
$^1/_4$ teaspoon dried oregano
1 tablespoon canola oil

In a bowl, combine the squash, pepper, scallions, garlic, parsley, salt, and white pepper. Mix in the egg. In a small bowl, combine the chick-pea flour, white flour, and baking powder, and stir it into the vegetable mixture. Let sit 15–20 minutes to allow the salt to draw liquid out of the vegetables. The batter should be thick, but moist, like that for potato pancakes. If the mixture is very wet, add a bit more flour. If it is too dry, add a little water. Mix in the basil and oregano.

Warm a large skillet or griddle over medium heat, add a teaspoon of the oil, and spoon the batter into the pan to make 3–4-inch rounds. Gently flatten the tops with the back of a spoon. Cook until firm and golden brown on bottom, about 3 minutes. Flip, and cook the other side. Transfer to a serving platter. Add another teaspoon of oil to the pan and continue until all the batter is cooked. Keep the fritters in a warm oven until ready to serve.

Sweet Pepper Pinto Bean Chili

Our bodies need vitamin C to help absorb the iron in beans. To let you get the most from the iron in this dish, we've included vitamin C–laden red sweet peppers, tomatoes, and chili powder.

2 tablespoons extra virgin olive oil
2 cloves garlic, minced
1¹/₂ cups minced onion (about 1¹/₂ medium onions)
1 cup diced red bell pepper
3 cups cooked pinto beans
2 cups drained canned tomatoes, liquid reserved

2 bay leaves
1 tablespoon chili powder, or to taste
1 teaspoon dried cumin
1 teaspoon dried oregano
Sea salt to taste

In a large skillet, heat the oil over medium heat. Add the garlic and sauté briefly, about 30 seconds. Lower the heat and add the onion. Cook until it begins to soften and change color, about 5 minutes. Add the pepper and cook 5 minutes longer. Add the beans, tomatoes, bay leaves, chili powder, cumin, oregano, and salt, plus a cup of the reserved tomato juice, bring to a boil. Lower the heat and simmer, uncovered, 30 minutes, adding more liquid as necessary. Remove bay leaves before serving.

Red Beans and Rice

Across the Louisiana bayous, red beans and rice are traditionally served for dinner on Monday nights. Here miso replaces the high-fat sausage or ham that usually flavors this dish. Serve with Louisiana Shrimp Stew (page 139).

2 cups red beans or kidney beans, soaked overnight
2 (6-inch) strips kombu
2 bay leaves
1 cup finely chopped onion (about 1 medium onion)
1/4 teaspoon dried thyme
2 cloves garlic, minced
1/4 cup minced fresh parsley
1 cup diced green bell pepper
3 tablespoons rice miso
4 cups cooked brown rice

Drain the beans. Place *kombu* on the bottom of 4-quart pressure cooker. Add the beans and bay leaves. Add 5 cups water and pressure-cook for 1 hour. The *kombu* will dissolve into the stock. After the pressure comes down, add the onion, thyme, garlic, parsley, and green pepper. Simmer in the open pressure cooker 15–20 minutes. Remove the bay leaves. Add the miso and simmer for 5 minutes more. For a thicker consistency, remove 1 cup of beans, mash them, and return them to the pot. If you do not have a pressure cooker, cook the beans with the *kombu* and bay leaves in a deep saucepan or Dutch oven for 2 hours, or until they are soft, then proceed as above.

Place a scoop of hot rice on each plate, spoon the beans over the rice, and serve.

Corn Bread Baked Beans

Somewhere between a tamale pie and chili with corn bread, this hefty casserole is a one-dish meal. Don't worry about the beans losing nutrients even though they are twice-cooked. Beans can be recooked for well over an hour and still retain 70–90 percent of their vitamins and minerals.

Baked Beans
2 cups kidney beans
3-inch-strip kombu
1½ teaspoons sea salt
1 bay leaf
¼ teaspoon cayenne pepper
½ teaspoon ground cumin

1 clove garlic, minced
1 cup diced onion (1 medium onion)
1 cup diced carrot (⅓ pound carrots)
1 cup diced celery (about 2 ribs)
¼ cup pitted and sliced green olives
1 tablespoon barley miso

Corn Bread
1 cup yellow cornmeal
2 tablespoons whole-wheat flour
¼ teaspoon sea salt
1½ teaspoons nonaluminum baking powder

2 tablespoons rice syrup
1 tablespoon corn oil

For beans: Soak the beans overnight. Drain and rinse. Combine the beans with 5 cups of water and the *kombu* in a pressure cooker. Bring up to pressure, reduce heat, and cook 50–60 minutes. Remove the cooker from the heat and let the pressure return to normal. Open the lid and add the salt, spices, and all vegetables except the olives. Simmer briskly, uncovered, 10 minutes. Add the olives and simmer 5 minutes longer. The mixture should be thick, like chili, but not dry. Remove the bay leaf. Stir in the miso.

Preheat oven to 425 degrees. Pour the bean mixture into a 3-quart heat-proof casserole.

For corn bread: In a medium bowl, combine the cornmeal, flour, salt, and baking powder. In a small bowl, thoroughly mix the rice syrup and corn oil with ⅔ cup of water. Add the wet ingredients to the cornmeal mixture and combine with as few strokes as possible. Spread the batter over the beans and bake, uncovered, until the corn bread is done, 20–25 minutes. The batter will partially sink into the beans, but it will rise as it cooks and form a golden crust.

Mexican Bean Spread

MAKES ABOUT 2 CUPS

Cumin and red onion zip up this lean alternative to refried beans. You can put this handy recipe together in your food processor in no time. Use it on tacos, or spread on nachos. We also like it topped with salsa and melted cheese to make a Tex-Mex grilled cheese sandwich.

2 cups cooked pinto beans, cooking water reserved
½ teaspoon sea salt (omit if beans are already salted)
1 tablespoon fresh lemon juice

1 teaspoon chili powder
⅛ teaspoon ground cumin
* Pinch garlic powder*
¼ teaspoon natural soy sauce
2 tablespoons minced red onion

In a blender or food processor, blend the beans, salt, lemon juice, chili powder, cumin, garlic powder, and soy sauce until smooth. If the mixture is too thick to blend, add a little bean cooking liquid or water. Stir in the onion and serve.

Mediterranean Bean Salad

The heart-healthy Mediterranean diet features a variety of salads made with white beans. If you don't have time to cook beans from scratch, canned cannellini beans, a kind of white kidney bean, will do nicely. Serve with Lemon Escarole Soup (page 25) some sliced, ripe tomatoes and crusty bread for a light but satisfying meal.

2 tablespoons extra virgin olive oil
1 tablespoon fresh lemon juice
2 tablespoons brown rice vinegar
1 clove garlic, minced
$1/4$ teaspoon sea salt
$1/8$ teaspoon black pepper

2 cups cooked navy beans, or Great Northern beans
$1/2$ cup diced onion ($1/2$ medium onion)
2 tablespoons minced fresh parsley
1 tablespoon minced fresh basil, or mint
Lettuce leaves, for garnish

In a small bowl, combine the oil, lemon juice, vinegar, garlic, salt, and pepper.

In a medium bowl, toss together the beans, onion, parsley, and basil or mint. Pour the dressing over the bean mixture and toss the salad. Let sit at least 30 minutes before serving.

Stored in a covered container and refrigerated, this salad will be at its best 1 or 2 days after it is made. To serve, line small bowls with leaf lettuce, fill with the beans, and garnish with parsley or a sprig of basil or mint.

7. Seafood

We love fish and feel it has a place in a diet that supports your well-being. If you follow the news, you have probably noticed that discussions about the benefits and risks of eating seafood flip back and forth faster than a freshly caught flounder. Before getting down to recipes for cooking them, we think it's important to look at the benefits and possible risks of including fish in your daily diet.

Seafood is an excellent source of protein and a much leaner one than red meat or poultry. Cod, haddock, and flatfish, such as sole and flounder, contain less than 1 percent fat, and 90 percent of that fat is unsaturated. Compare this with skinless white-meat chicken, the next-leanest animal protein, which contains about 1.25 percent fat, only 75 percent of which is unsaturated. In addition, seafood is low in cholesterol and calories.

Seafood is also a good source of vitamin B_{12}, iodine, phosphorus, selenium, and zinc. Most important, it provides polyunsaturated fats known as omega-3s, which have anticlotting properties that protect against heart attack and high blood pressure. Studies show that just two servings of fish per week can reduce the risk of heart disease.

Omega-3 fatty acids have been shown to lower artery-damaging LDL cholesterol, raise helpful HDL cholesterol, lower blood pressure, and protect against strokes by making the blood less prone to clotting. Omega-3s may also have the ability to help control inflammatory conditions such as arthritis, psoriasis, and ulcerative colitis.

One of the most important contributions of fish oils is EPA, or *eicosapentaenoic acid.* EPA is an omega-3 oil and an essential component of cell membranes and hormonelike substances called *prostaglandins,* which work throughout the body as microregulators. EPAs and similar nutrients are required for the optimal functioning of a whole array of body processes.

As we learn more about nutrition and the human body, we discover modern research often merely reinforces traditional properties ascribed to foods in folklore. In particular, shellfish, especially oysters, appears high on lists of foods supposed to have aphrodisiac qualities, while fish is often referred to as "brain food." Actually, seafood is a source of tyrosine, an amino acid the body converts into dopamine and norepinephrine. These two chemicals help enhance mental alertness. Fish provides choline, which improves memory and is a relaxant. And as a source of zinc, a mineral essential to the production of sperm and male hormones, seafood like herring, oysters, and clams are unsurpassed.

Along with these virtues, there is no question that eating seafood can carry risks, though most illnesses attributed to consuming it are not serious and actually affect very few people. Eating raw shellfish can lead to gastroenteritis. Cooking kills the bacteria that cause this problem, though the best way to avoid contaminated clams, oysters, and mussels is knowing the people you buy them from. Fish can carry parasites such as tapeworm and roundworm. Freezing to 20 degrees below zero, which can be done commercially, kills these parasites and many potentially harmful bacteria as well. If you eat sushi or sashimi or seviche, you should ask whether the fish you will consume has been appropriately frozen. If the restaurant where you are eating or the store where you shop can't tell you, you may want to skip it. When tuna, swordfish, and shark come from waters polluted with heavy metals, such as mercury, or with dioxin, pesticides, or PCBs, in the case of bluefish and striped bass in the Northeastern United States, the level of these chemicals in their flesh may exceed what the FDA defines as safe. Your best protection is limiting how often you eat such fish and not constantly eating fish caught in the same area. Buying fish from a supermarket or fish store makes this unlikely in most parts of the country anyway.

Ciguatoxin and scrombotoxin can also cause illness if you eat fish containing elevated levels of these substances. This problem is rather rare. The best way to avoid ciguatoxin, which is generated in algaelike organisms consumed and passed up the food chain to larger fish, is not to eat grouper, barracuda, amberjack, or red snapper from the tropics. Scrombotoxin develops when scromboid fish such as tuna, mackerel, bluefish, and mahi-mahi are left out at high temperatures for a long time. To avoid scromboid poisoning, do not eat fish that appears spoiled or smells bad—a wise practice with any seafood. Also avoid eating scromboids caught by recreational fishers, who may not have kept the fish properly chilled.

Until we have a national program for the inspection of fish, observe these basic guidelines to minimize the risks:

· Know your source. This is particularly important if you eat shellfish.
· Consider avoiding shellfish during the warm summer months. If you feel concerned at all, don't eat it.
· Eat a variety of fish. You are not likely to take in excessive amounts of mercury unless you eat tainted fish repeatedly. If you are pregnant or nursing, do not eat shark, swordfish, or tuna regularly.
· Avoid fish caught in tropical waters, particularly large grouper, red snapper, and barracuda. Do not eat the roe from any of these fish.
· If dark-fleshed fish looks questionable, do not eat it. Pick a different fish.

Despite the potential hazards, statistics from the FDA and Centers for Disease Control indicate that there are far fewer reported illnesses associated with seafood than with chicken. Chicken is responsible for approximately one illness per 25,000 servings, and seafood for only one illness per 250,000 servings. Exclude clams, oysters, and other bivalve mollusks that are commonly eaten raw, and these figures drop to one illness per 5 million servings. Those odds should be long enough to reassure fish lovers and everyone who wants the benefits of eating seafood.

When deciding to eat seafood, select whatever is freshest at the market. Shellfish should be alive, with the exception of scallops. Whole fish should feel firm and spring back when you press it with a finger. The gills should be clean and bright red. The eyes should be flush with the surface of the head and clear. However, if they are cloudy, it may simply indicate that the fish has been buried in ice. Look for fish with glossy scales that cling tightly and feel slightly slimy. This mucus coating helps protect fish from invasion by bacteria and disintegrates after the fish has been out of water for a while. Fillets should feel firm and look translucent. Whether buying a whole fish or fillets, follow your nose. Fresh fish smells clean and faintly like the sea; avoid anything with a fishy odor. Finally, first pick the fish, then choose a recipe. If you do want to make a particular recipe from this book, most are flexible enough to work well with a variety of fish.

When you buy fish, get it home and into the refrigerator as quickly as possible. If you are not using it immediately, place the fish in a plastic bag. Put the bag on crushed ice in a bowl. Cover it with more ice, and store in the coldest part of your refrigerator. Store live shellfish in an open plastic or paper bag, with a wet paper towel to keep them moist.

Whether serving seafood broiled, baked, poached, steamed, or grilled, avoid overcooking it. As a general rule, allow 10 minutes per inch of thickness for white flatfish, a bit longer for salmon and firmer-fleshed kinds. Fish is done when the flesh just loses its translucence and flakes easily with a fork. Remember that fish continues cooking after it has been removed from the heat.

Cod Fillets en Papillote with Sun-dried Tomatoes

"En papillote" refers to foods cooked in an envelope of parchment or aluminum foil. This cooking method keeps in the juices and gives succulent results. Here, sun-dried tomatoes and green pepper add sweetness and color while complementing the delicate flavor of meaty fresh cod. You can use other thick, mild fishes such as halibut or turbot. Serve with Steamed Broccoli with Walnut Miso (page 109).

$1/3$ cup minced oil-packed sun-dried
tomatoes, plus $1^1/2$ tablespoons oil from
tomatoes
1 clove garlic, minced
1 teaspoon brown rice vinegar
3 tablespoons minced red onion
$1^1/2$ tablespoons minced fresh parsley
$1/4$ teaspoon dried basil

$1/4$ teaspoon dried marjoram
Extra virgin olive oil
1 lemon, cut into thin rounds
4 cod fillets (about $1^1/2$ pounds)
$1/4$ teaspoon sea salt
$1/8$ teaspoon black pepper
1 green bell pepper, seeded and cut into
thin rings

Preheat oven to 425 degrees. Cut four 12-inch-square pieces of cooking parchment or aluminum foil and set aside.

In a small bowl, combine the tomatoes and their oil, garlic, vinegar, onion, parsley, basil, and marjoram, and mix well.

Brush the surface of the parchment or foil with the olive oil, and arrange a layer of lemon slices at the center of each. Rinse the fillets, pat dry, lightly salt the bottoms, and place on the lemon slices. Brush top and sides of fish lightly with oil, and sprinkle with salt and pepper. Arrange the green pepper rings side by side on the fish. Fill the rings and any area of the fish's upper surface with the tomato mixture.

To wrap, brush the edges of the parchment paper with water. (Omit this step if using foil.) Bring top and bottom edges of the paper or foil up together over fish and fold over at least twice, making ½-inch folds. Fold left and right ends similarly. Don't wrap too snugly; each parcel needs room inside for steam to build.

Place the parcels on a baking sheet, and bake for 15 minutes for each inch of thickness of the fish.

If using parchment, the edges should be puffed and browned when the fish is done. The parcels should be served as they are; diners slit them open with their knives, releasing puffs of steam carrying the bouquet of fish and herbs. The paper and lemon rounds are discarded.

If using foil, carefully unwrap the packages, transfer the fish, without the lemon slices, to plates, and serve immediately.

Portuguese Fish Stew

SERVES 6

Orange zest, saffron, and fennel seeds add sunny Mediterranean flavors to this golden fish dish. Serve it with crusty bread for dipping in the juices.

2 tablespoons olive oil
2 large onions, diced
4 cloves garlic, minced
¼ teaspoon sea salt
½ teaspoon ground fennel seeds
    Pinch ground cloves
½ teaspoon saffron threads dissolved in 2 tablespoons boiling water
1 (28-ounce) can whole peeled tomatoes, drained, seeded, and chopped, liquid reserved

3 medium potatoes, peeled and cut into chunks
1 small butternut squash, peeled, seeded, and cut into chunks
1 bay leaf
1 3-inch strip orange zest
1½ pounds codfish steak, 1 inch thick, rinsed, dried, and cut into chunks
1 tablespoon fresh lemon juice
    Freshly ground black pepper to taste
¼ cup minced fresh parsley, for garnish

In a Dutch oven, heat the olive oil. Add the onions, garlic, and salt. Stir until onions and garlic are coated with the oil. Cover pot tightly and sweat the onions and garlic over medium heat for 30 minutes, until they are very soft, stirring occasionally. Add the fennel seeds and cloves, and cook 1 minute before adding the saffron, tomatoes, potatoes, squash, bay leaf, orange zest, and 2 cups of water.

Cook, partially covered, over medium heat until the vegetables are soft, about 20 minutes. Add the fish and cook until tender and flaky, about 5 minutes.

Season with the lemon juice, salt, and pepper. Remove the zest strip and the bay leaf. Garnish with the parsley.

Steamed Salmon Piccante

SERVES 4

The Asian quartet of sake, soy, ginger, and garlic makes a perfect accompaniment to the sweet taste of salmon. If cooking fish makes you uncomfortable, this dish is a perfect choice: all it requires is steaming the fish over boiling water. Halibut and swordfish can also be used to make this dish.

4 fish steaks or fillets (about 1¹/₂ pounds)
¹/₂ teaspoon sea salt
2 tablespoons sake
1 tablespoon natural soy sauce
2 teaspoons peeled and minced ginger

2 teaspoons minced garlic
Juice of 1 lemon, plus 1 lemon cut into wedges, for garnish
Dash cayenne pepper

Rinse the fish, pat dry, and sprinkle lightly with the salt. Arrange the fish in a heatproof 8-inch-square baking dish. In a small bowl, combine the sake, soy sauce, ginger, and garlic, and pour over the fish. Squeeze the juice of one of the lemons over the fish and sprinkle with the cayenne.

Set the baking dish on a rack in a large stockpot over boiling water and steam until the fish is tender and flaky, 8–12 minutes. Serve hot with lemon wedges.

Jamaican Baked Fish Fillets

The bright taste of lime juice complements the richness of oily fish like mackerel. The bite of the chili peppers in the sauce provides an intriguing counterpoint against the coolness of cucumber, the tang of rice vinegar, and the tropical flavor of allspice. Try bluefish in this recipe if you cannot find mackerel in the market.

Canola oil
6 fillets of mackerel, bluefish, or any kind of fresh oily fish (about 2 pounds)
¼ cup fresh lime juice (about 2 limes)
1 teaspoon sea salt
Black pepper

1 cucumber, cut into long, thin strips
2 medium onions, sliced thin
3 jalapeño peppers, seeded and minced
1 cup brown rice vinegar
2 tablespoons whole allspice berries

Preheat oven to 400 degrees. Oil bottom of a covered heatproof baking dish.

Rub the fish with the lime juice, and sprinkle it with ½ teaspoon of the salt and the pepper. Place the fish in the baking dish, cover, and bake until tender and flaky, about 15 minutes.

Place the cucumber, onions, jalapeños, vinegar, allspice, and remaining ½ teaspoon salt in a medium, nonreactive saucepan. Bring to a boil, reduce heat, and simmer 10 minutes. Pour over cooked fish and serve.

Shrimp Biryani

A *biryani* is a rice pilaf. This one is particularly festive, with colorful shrimp set against saffron rice. The blend of Indian spices adds an exquisite fragrance. Use an attractive baking dish, and bring this dish straight from the oven to the table.

2 pounds medium shrimp
2 large onions
6 cloves garlic, peeled
  2-inch-piece fresh ginger, peeled
1/4 cup lemon juice
3 tablespoons canola oil
1 tablespoon whole cloves
1 tablespoon black peppercorns
1 tablespoon fennel seeds
1 tablespoon black mustard seeds
1 tablespoon coriander seeds

1 tablespoon cumin seeds
1 teaspoon sea salt
1 cup plain yogurt
1 1/2 cups basmati rice
1/3 cup plain soy beverage
1/2 teaspoon saffron threads
1/2 cup golden raisins
1 cup roasted unsalted cashews, for garnish
1 hard-boiled egg, thinly sliced, for garnish

Peel, devein, and rinse the shrimp. Quarter 1 onion and place in a food processor with the garlic and ginger. Add the lemon juice, pulse a few times, and pour the mixture into a bowl. Thinly slice the other onion.

In a heavy skillet, heat the oil, add the sliced onion and all the spices, and sauté over medium heat until the onions are tender, about 10 minutes. Remove from heat and stir in the yogurt. Add to the ginger mixture and mix well. Cover and refrigerate until needed. It will keep up to 2 days.

About 1 hour before serving, preheat oven to 350 degrees. Bring 4 cups of water to a boil in a medium saucepan. Reduce heat, add the rice, and simmer 10 minutes. Drain in a strainer. Place the shrimp, with the sauce mixture, in a heat-proof serving dish, gently pour in the rice, and smooth the top.

In a small saucepan, bring the soy beverage and saffron threads to a simmer. Remove from heat and let steep for 2 minutes. Pour carefully, in streaks, over the rice. Sprinkle the raisins evenly over the rice. Bake, covered, 35 minutes.

Serve in the baking dish or in a bowl, decorated with the roasted cashews and egg slices.

Orange Roughy with Citrus Vinaigrette

Orange roughy is a mild-flavored fish that contains the least amount of cholesterol of all seafood. The vegetables in this dish make it particularly appealing and almost a complete meal in itself. Since it's also a quick dish to prepare, serve it when you are having company and time is short. All you need to add is some cooked rice on the side.

VINAIGRETTE

- 1 tablespoon orange juice
- 2 tablespoons lemon juice
- 2 teaspoons grated lemon zest
- 1 teaspoon prepared yellow mustard
- $1/4$ cup extra virgin olive oil
- $1/4$ teaspoon sea salt
- Pinch white pepper

FISH AND VEGETABLES

- 4 green beans, cut on the diagonal into $1/4$-inch-wide strips
- 1 small carrot, cut into matchsticks
- $1^1/2$ pounds orange roughy fillets
- Pinch sea salt
- Pinch white pepper
- 1 scallion, sliced thin
- 1 square-inch lemon zest, cut into very thin strips

Preheat oven to 400 degrees. Oil a baking dish large enough to fit the fish in one layer.

For vinaigrette: In a small bowl, whisk or beat the vinaigrette ingredients together until they are blended.

For fish and vegetables: In a small pot of lightly salted boiling water, cook green beans, uncovered, 2 minutes. With a slotted spoon, remove beans and plunge into cold water to set the color and stop the cooking. Drain. Repeat with the carrots.

Rinse the fish fillets, pat dry with a paper towel, and season lightly with salt and pepper. Arrange the fish in the oiled baking dish. Cover tightly with a lid or aluminum foil. Bake until the fish flakes and is no longer translucent inside, about 10 minutes. Transfer the fish to warmed individual plates or a platter. Sprinkle with the green beans, carrots, scallion, and lemon zest. Spoon vinaigrette over all and serve.

Baked Sole with Leeks and Shiitake Mushrooms

SERVES 4

A study in contrasts, this low-fat dish resonates with the warm flavors of leeks and shiitakes, the warmth of ginger, and a top note of sweet dill. It's a perfect choice for a cozy winter dinner. If you like, try salmon in place of the sole.

1¼ pounds fillet of sole
1 tablespoon extra virgin olive oil
6–8 slices ginger, peeled and cut very thin on the diagonal
½ cup semi-dry white wine
2 tablespoons chopped fresh dill
¼ teaspoon plus pinch sea salt
⅛ teaspoon ground white pepper
2 tablespoons fresh lemon juice

1 leek, white part only, slit lengthwise to center, rinsed well, and cut crosswise into ¼-inch slices
6–8 fresh shiitake mushrooms, stems discarded and caps sliced thin
Pinch cayenne pepper
Lemon wedges, for seasoning fish at the table

Rinse the fish in cold water, and lightly pat dry with paper towels. Oil a shallow baking dish with 1 teaspoon of the oil. Arrange the ginger slices in the prepared baking dish and lay the fish on the ginger.

Preheat oven to 425 degrees. In a small bowl, combine the wine, dill, ¼ teaspoon salt, pepper, and lemon juice, and pour over the fish. Marinate 30 minutes, spooning the liquid over the fillets once or twice.

(continued on next page)

Baked Sole with Leeks and Shiitake Mushrooms (*cont.*)

In a small skillet over medium heat, heat the remaining oil. Add the leeks and mushrooms and a pinch of sea salt, and sauté 3–4 minutes. Sprinkle the fish with the cayenne, and arrange the mushrooms and leeks over and around the fish. Bake, covered, until the fish flakes and is tender, about 15 minutes. Serve immediately with lemon wedges.

Grilled Fish with Salsa Verde

Salmon and halibut both hold together well and are thick and moist enough to stand up to the heat of grilling. This Italian sauce, a blend of aromatic herbs sparked with lemon juice and a touch of anchovy, goes perfectly with the richness of either fish. Leftovers taste so delicious you may want to cook up extra portions of this dish just to be sure you have some.

SALSA

1 heaping tablespoon pine nuts
3 tablespoons finely chopped fresh basil
1½ tablespoons finely chopped fresh parsley

1 rounded teaspoon minced garlic
1 teaspoon fresh lemon juice
1 teaspoon finely chopped anchovy

½ tablespoon extra virgin olive oil, plus extra for basting
4 fillets salmon or halibut (about 1½ pounds)

Sea salt
Freshly ground black pepper

For the salsa: In a small dry skillet over medium-low heat, toast the pine nuts, stirring continuously until fragrant, about 3 minutes. Remove from pan, cool, and chop.

Prepare a grill, or preheat broiler. Oil the grill rack or a baking sheet, if broiling the fish.

In a small bowl, combine the pine nuts, basil, parsley, garlic, lemon juice, and anchovy and mix. Add the ½ tablespoon oil and mix well. The consistency will be like pesto or a bit thinner.

For the fish: Rinse the fish and pat dry. If you are cooking fillets with skin, make a few shallow, diagonal slashes in the skin to prevent the fish from curling. Brush with olive oil and sprinkle lightly with salt and pepper. If using fillets with skin, place flesh side toward the heat first, so you can turn the fish only once and end up with the skin side down to serve. If the fillets taper to very thin ends, fold ends under so fish cooks evenly.

Cook the fish until tender and flaky, 8–10 minutes per inch of thickness. Turn the fillets after half the estimated time, and baste with oil.

To serve: Transfer the cooked fish to warmed individual serving plates or a platter, top each portion with a generous spoonful of the salsa verde, and serve.

Grilled Salmon Steaks with Red Onion

SERVES 4

This is one of the simplest fish dishes we know, but it tastes so good no one will guess how easy it is to make. Grilling caramelizes the sugar in the onions, bringing out their natural sweetness. Serve with a tossed salad and warm pita bread. Pass Honeyed Teriyaki Sauce (page 162) on the side.

½ cup canola oil
¼ cup natural soy sauce
2 tablespoons rice syrup
2 medium red onions, sliced into
  ¼-inch-thick half-moons

2 pounds salmon steaks
Fresh chives, for garnish

Prepare a hot charcoal or wood fire, or heat the broiler. In a small bowl, combine the oil, soy sauce, and rice syrup. Using a pastry brush, brush the onion slices and salmon with this mixture. Grill the onions 5 minutes each side. Grill the salmon steaks 3 minutes each side, until no longer translucent in the center. They should be firm and springy to the touch. Garnish with the chives.

Seafood Citrus Ceviche

SERVES 6

Ceviche is a Latin American dish. The acid in the citrus juices "cooks" the seafood. A garnish of fresh fruit slices adds color. This is a refreshing summertime dish to serve for lunch or dinner.

1 pound scallops, or a combination of scallops, shrimp, and white fish, such as halibut, scrod, or haddock
½ cup fresh lime juice (about 4 limes)
3 tablespoons fresh lemon juice
6 tablespoons fresh orange juice
¼ cup mirin
½ teaspoon plus pinch sea salt
2 tablespoons minced onion

2 tablespoons minced red bell pepper
½ teaspoon minced jalapeño pepper
1 tablespoon extra virgin olive oil
Lettuce leaves to serve under fish
2 sprigs cilantro, stems removed, for garnish
Slices of lime, lemon, and orange, for garnish

Rinse the scallops under cold running water and drain. Cut large sea scallops in halves or thirds, and remove the heel. Leave small bay scallops whole. If using shrimp, peel, devein, and rinse. Remove skin from fish, cut into 1-inch cubes, and rinse.

In a small bowl, combine the lime, lemon, and orange juices. Add the *mirin* and ½ teaspoon of salt, and stir. Place the seafood in a nonreactive bowl or casserole, and cover with the juices. Refrigerate at least 5 hours, or overnight. The seafood will become firm and solid white in color.

In a small bowl, combine the onion, peppers, olive oil, and pinch of salt. Drain two-thirds of the marinade from the seafood and discard. Add the vegetables to the seafood and mix. Marinate 1 hour more.

To serve, drain the seafood and arrange on a bed of lettuce. Garnish with the cilantro leaves and fruit slices.

Louisiana Shrimp Stew

"First, make the roux . . ." starts many a Cajun recipe. Here, cholesterol-free sesame oil takes the place of the bacon drippings traditionally used for the roux, a blend of fat and flour. Using the shrimp shells to make a stock adds even more flavor to this feast of a dish. Serve with Aromatic Basmati Rice (page 42).

$1/2$ cup sesame oil
$3/4$ cup unbleached white flour
1 pound medium shrimp
1 tablespoon extra virgin olive oil
2 cups thinly sliced onions
1 cup diced green bell pepper
2 cups thinly sliced celery

2 teaspoons sea salt, or to taste
3 cloves garlic, minced
1 cup diced red bell pepper
1 teaspoon dried thyme
1 cup chopped scallions
1 cup chopped fresh parsley

Make a roux by heating the sesame oil in a heavy skillet over medium heat. Sprinkle the flour over the oil and stir continuously, until the roux begins to brown. Reduce the heat to medium-low and stir often, until the roux turns the color of peanut butter, about 20–25 minutes. Remove from heat and cool, stirring frequently. Pour off a little of the separated oil.

Peel and devein the shrimp, reserving the shells. Refrigerate the shrimp until needed.

In a medium saucepan, bring 4 cups of water to a simmer and cook the shrimp shells for 15 minutes. Drain, reserving the stock. In a heavy soup pot, heat the olive oil and sauté the onions, green pepper, and celery until crisp-tender, about 5 minutes. Add the roux and salt, and stir. Slowly add the shrimp stock, 1 cup at a time, mixing thoroughly after each addition. Add the garlic, red pepper, and thyme. Simmer, stirring occasionally, until thick, 30–40 minutes. Add the shrimp, scallions, and parsley. Simmer 7–10 minutes longer. Adjust seasonings to taste and serve hot over warm rice.

8. Salads and Dressings

Does someone you know think salads are rabbit food? For them, does it take a dousing of creamy dressing just to make a plate of fresh greens edible? Here is a new look at salads and dressings that are varied, good-tasting, colorful, and full of healthful nutrition. They range from simple side salads to sophisticated compositions no one would ever pigeonhole as "health food." We also offer dressings made with ingredients like miso and tofu, balsamic vinegar and extra virgin olive oil, that bring solid nutritional benefits along with great taste.

Eating at least one salad every day is helpful if you want to get your full share of the vitamins, minerals, dietary fiber, and other nutrients important for your health. It's easy to do when you think about all the ingredients and combinations you can use. These recipes, along with others scattered throughout this book, show how many different types of salads are possible, from combinations of leafy greens to hefty mixes of grains or pasta with vegetables and cheese. Nonvegetarians can even make salads, such as our Avocodo with Shrimp and Pasta Salad (page 147), that draw on all of the four basic food groups.

If you think making salads is too much bother, consider the first recipe in this chapter. It's a simple cucumber and tomato salad tossed with a brown rice vinegar dressing. You can put this salad and its dressing together in just ten minutes. But the gentle flavor of the naturally fermented rice vinegar sets off the other ingredients to perfection. A more elegant salad, a combination of endive and fresh raspberries with a hazelnut vinaigrette, may take fifteen minutes of your time to prepare. And it's such a memorable combination of tastes and textures that no one will think about the generous portions of vitamin C, *ellagic acid* (a natural substance, found in berries, that scientists believe may help prevent certain kinds of cancer), and a bunch of other useful nutrients they are getting. There are also other salads in this chapter that can be prepared in reasonable amounts of time. A number of them can also be made ahead and kept until you are ready for them.

The benefits of a salad can get lost if you drown it in an oily vinaigrette or one of the thick cream dressings Americans favor. Every tablespoon of oil you pour over a healthful, low-calorie, fiber-rich salad adds 135 calories, 15 grams of fat, and possibly, globs of cholesterol that you do not need. Commercially made salad dressings are usually loaded with sodium and empty calories from sugar as well.

Some people cut down on the fat in their salad dressing by using bottled fat-free products with a list of ingredients that reads like a chemistry lesson. Others buy oil-free dressings that taste like a bottle of vinegar and are made with artificial sweeteners. We offer a different approach.

If you want a creamy salad dressing, use one like our Green Empress Dressing (page 154). Its richness comes from a combination of creamy tofu and delicious miso. Both supply protein and useful vitamins and minerals while making the dressing thick and satisfying. Or try our New Potato Salad with Tahini Tarragon Dressing (page 150). The tahini adds an extra measure of calcium and iron to this dressing, along with its nutty flavor.

Our love affair with fresh fruits and vegetables is no secret. We want to help you discover ways to enjoy adding more of them to your diet every day. Our readers tell us these salad recipes have shown them how and inspired them to try a variety of foods they had not used before.

Cucumber Tomato Salad

When cherry tomatoes are good, they explode with flavor. No wonder they are so popular, particularly during winter months when other tomatoes tend to be hard and bland, as a way to satisfy our need for vitamin C. Make enough of this salad to have leftovers marinated in the dressing overnight, and you'll have a delicious sandwich filling.

SALAD
10 cherry tomatoes
1 cucumber

4 leaves basil

DRESSING
3 tablespoons extra virgin olive oil
2 tablespoons brown rice vinegar

$1/4$ teaspoon sea salt
$1/8$ teaspoon black pepper

For the salad: Cut the tomatoes in half. Cut the cucumber in half lengthwise, and then cut into $1/4$-inch-thick half-moons. Chop the basil coarsely.

For the dressing: In a small bowl, whisk together the oil, vinegar, salt, and pepper. Put the salad in a serving bowl and toss with the dressing.

Blood Orange and Lemon Salad

Now that blood oranges are being grown in California, look for them in supermarkets during the winter, when citrus fruits are in season. The vivid color in the skin and flesh of these oranges comes from autho cyanins; however, these pigments don't make blood oranges richer in beta carotene than other oranges. If you can't find blood oranges, use sweet navels instead to make this vibrant salad. Serve with Shrimp Biryani (page 133).

4 *blood oranges*
2 *lemons*
$^1/_2$ *small red onion, sliced into*
  $^1/_8$-inch-thick rings

2 *tablespoons chopped fresh basil*
$^1/_8$ *teaspoon freshly ground black pepper*
2 *tablespoons extra virgin olive oil*

Working over a bowl to catch the juices, remove peels and pith from the oranges and lemons. Slice them into thin rounds, and remove the seeds. Put the fruit slices and onion rings in the bowl containing the juices. Add the basil, pepper, and olive oil, and toss lightly. Allow to stand at room temperature 2 hours. Serve from the bowl or arrange on individual plates.

Kiwi, Orange, and Watercress Salad

Some combinations not only taste good, they also make sense nutritionally. Here, the citrus fruit provides vitamin C, which helps the body absorb the iron in the watercress. A touch of sweetness in the dressing plays up the flavors of both the cress and the fruit. Serve with Grilled Salmon Steaks with Red Onion (page 137).

1 large navel orange, peeled and pith removed
1 large pink or red grapefruit, peel and pith removed
2 tablespoons umeboshi *vinegar*
1/8 teaspoon cayenne pepper

2 teaspoons maple syrup, or clover honey
2 tablespoons walnut oil, or light sesame oil
1 bunch watercress
3 large kiwi fruit, peeled

Halve the orange lengthwise, then cut across into very thin half-rounds. Repeat with the grapefruit, removing any seeds. Place both in a bowl. Add to bowl any juice from cut fruit left on cutting board.

In a small bowl, mix the *umeboshi* vinegar, cayenne, and syrup or honey. Add the oil, and drain in the juice that has accumulated in the bowl of the cut fruits.

On individual serving plates or one large platter, arrange the watercress around the edges. Just inside the watercress, overlap the slices of grapefruit and orange. Cut the kiwi fruit into thin rounds and arrange in the center of the plate.

Cover and chill. Drizzle on salad dressing just before serving.

Endive Raspberry Salad

Bitter endive and tart-sweet raspberries are unexpected partners in this jewel-colored salad. Serve it after a rich main course such as grilled salmon or creamy Pasta Primavera (page 61), when the digestive stimulation of the bitter greens can be especially appreciated.

4–8 *curly endive leaves*
  1 *cup fresh raspberries*
 10 *hazelnuts, lightly roasted and chopped*
  2 *tablespoons extra virgin olive oil*

1 *tablespoon raspberry vinegar*
1 *clove garlic, pressed*
  Pinch sea salt

Tear the greens into bite-size pieces and arrange on individual salad plates. Arrange the berries on the greens, and sprinkle the hazelnuts on top. In a small bowl, mix the oil, vinegar, garlic, and salt. Drizzle over the salads just before serving.

Avocado with Shrimp and Pasta Salad

This luxurious salad includes foods from every major group on the U.S. Department of Agriculture's Food Guide Pyramid. If shrimp are too expensive, canned tuna fish tossed with an extra dollop of the spicy Mustard-Cayenne Sauce can take its place.

 4 large iceberg lettuce leaves
 2 ripe avocados, peeled, pitted, and halved
12 jumbo shrimp, cooked, shelled, and deveined
 4 tablespoons barbecue sauce
1–2 large endives, leaves separated and rinsed

 1 cup canned mandarin orange sections, drained
 3 cups cooked pasta shells, or macaroni
 4 tablespoons currants
    Mustard Cayenne Sauce (page 171)

Place one or two leaves of lettuce on each of four dinner plates. Put half of an avocado, with the hollow facing up, in the center. Arrange three shrimp in each avocado half. Let the tails dangle out as in shrimp cocktail, and apply a dab of barbecue sauce to the center of each shrimp. Arrange the endive leaves around the avocado like points of a star. Sprinkle the orange sections and pasta in and around the hollows of the endive leaves. Scatter a few currants on each finished plate. Dress with Mustard Cayenne Sauce.

Raita
(Spiced Yogurt Salad)

Raita (rah-EE-ta) is an Indian dish made with yogurt that is served to cool the mouth after the heat of spicy dishes. This vegetable-studded version is a good way to add vitamin C and calcium to a meal. If you cannot find fresh coriander at your supermarket, look for it at an Asian or Hispanic food store. Serve with Kabuli Chole (page 115) or Spinach Bombay with Tofu Cheese (page 84).

16 ounces plain yogurt
1½ cups seeded and diced tomatoes
1 cup diced red onion
1½ cups peeled, seeded, and diced cucumber

⅔ cup chopped fresh coriander, or parsley
1 teaspoon sea salt
1 tablespoon Garam Masala *(page 240)*
½ teaspoon turmeric

Place all ingredients in a bowl and mix thoroughly. Chill well before serving.

String Bean and Chick-pea Salad with Dilled Soy Mayonnaise

Dill, shallots, and fresh chives are a perfect way to perk up the bland flavor of beans. Canned chick-peas can make putting this salad together even easier. The eggless mayonnaise dressing for this salad is prepared in the blender. It can also be used to make a delicious coleslaw.

SALAD
1 pound string beans
2 cups cooked chick-peas

1/4 cup minced shallots
1/2 cup chopped chives

MAYONNAISE
1/4 cup plain soy beverage
1/4 cup light extra virgin olive oil
2 tablespoons minced fresh dill, or
  1 teaspoon dried

1 tablespoon brown rice vinegar
1/4 teaspoon sea salt
1/8 teaspoon dry mustard

For salad: Trim the string beans, cut into 2-inch lengths, and steam them until they are tender-crisp, about 5 minutes. Immediately plunge the cooked beans into cold water to stop the cooking and maintain the color. In a large bowl, combine the cooled beans, chick-peas, shallots, and chives.

For mayonnaise: In a blender, combine all the mayonnaise ingredients and blend until smooth and thick. If the dressing is too thin, pour additional oil in a slow stream into the blender with the motor running.

Mix dressing with salad, and chill for an hour or longer before serving.

New Potato Salad with Tahini Tarragon Dressing

SERVES 8–10

Potatoes are usually considered a carbohydrate, but they are also a moderate source of protein. A blend of fresh herbs and red onion gives bright flavors to this salad. Tahini adds calcium to the creamy, dairy-free dressing. Serve with Steamed Salmon Piccante (page 131).

3 pounds new potatoes
2 cups fresh peas, blanched and rinsed in cold water
1 cup minced red onion
2 tablespoons minced fresh parsley
3 tablespoons minced fresh tarragon

1 tablespoon minced fresh savory
1 tablespoon minced fresh oregano
Tahini Tarragon Dressing (recipe follows)
Lettuce leaves or radicchio, for garnish
Dash freshly ground white pepper

In a large pot, place the potatoes and cover with lightly salted water. Place over medium-high heat and boil until tender but firm, 15-20 minutes. Don't overcook the potatoes or they will fall apart. Pour the potatoes into a colander and rinse until cool. Drain, place the potatoes in a bowl, and refrigerate until cold.

Cut potatoes into thirds or any size you prefer, and place in a large bowl. Add the peas, onion, parsley, tarragon, savory, and oregano. Mix lightly to blend. Pour the dressing over the potatoes and herbs and toss gently. Serve on lettuce leaves or radicchio with a crowning dash of fresh pepper.

Tahini Tarragon Dressing

1 tablespoon minced garlic
½ cup fresh lemon juice
½ cup extra virgin olive oil
½ teaspoon sea salt

⅛ teaspoon freshly ground white pepper
1 teaspoon bottled hot sauce
3 tablespoons tahini
2 teaspoons Dijon mustard

In a small bowl, whisk together the dressing ingredients.

Mediterranean Salad with Balsamic Vinaigrette

For this leafy salad, we have used balsamic vinegar and fresh herbs to add sparkle to the classic vinaigrette dressing. In place of croutons, cauliflower and snow peas give extra crunch. They also bring an extra helping of vitamins C and A. Serve with Italian Baked Polenta Squares (page 50).

$^1/_2$ medium head cauliflower, separated
  into florets
20 snow peas, or sugar snap peas
 6 cups bite-size pieces mixed salad greens
  (lettuce, spinach, radicchio, escarole,
  arugula, dandelion, etc.)

$^1/_4$ medium red onion, slivered
 2 tablespoons pitted and sliced black
  olives
  Balsamic Vinaigrette (recipe follows)

Steam or parboil the cauliflower in or over lightly salted boiling water until crisp-tender, 2–3 minutes. Drain and cool to room temperature. In a saucepan, parboil the peas 1 minute, drain, and immediately transfer to a bowl of cold water to preserve their color. Cool and drain.

Divide the salad greens among four individual bowls or plates, and arrange the onion, cauliflower, peas, and olives on top.

Add the dressing immediately before serving, or pass it on the side.

Balsamic Vinaigrette

2/3 cup extra virgin olive oil
3–4 tablespoons balsamic vinegar
1 clove garlic, minced
1/2 teaspoon sea salt

1/4 teaspoon freshly ground pepper
1/2 teaspoon dry mustard
1 tablespoon minced fresh basil, dill, or parsley

In a small bowl, combine the oil, vinegar, garlic, salt, pepper, mustard, and basil, dill, or parsley. Beat vigorously with a fork or whisk. Or put ingredients in a jar, cover, and shake well.

Amasake Dressing

Every time we finish the salad served in our favorite Japanese restaurant, we wish we could take some of the tangy dressing home. Here, *amasake,* a creamy, thick beverage made from rice, is the base for a dressing that comes close. It can be found in natural food stores. Serve this dressing in place of fat-laden Italian and ranch-style dressings. The flavor goes particularly well with crisp romaine lettuce and shredded carrots.

1/2 cup amasake
2 tablespoons sesame oil
2 tablespoons extra virgin olive oil

1/4 cup brown rice vinegar
1 tablespoon red miso
1 clove garlic, minced

In a blender, process all the ingredients until smooth. Serve with tossed salads or pasta salads. Garnish with croutons, toasted seeds, or chopped nuts.

Green Empress Dressing

You can enjoy this nutritious dressing without a twinge of guilt. True, avocados are high in fat, but it is monounsaturated fat and not the kind loaded with empty calories. The tofu adds calcium, while garlic and onions contribute cancer-fighting benefits, and parsley adds iron and vitamin A. Crisp greens or diced cold chicken are perfect partners for this dressing.

1/3 pound soft tofu
1 ripe avocado, peeled and pitted
1 clove garlic, pressed
2 tablespoons chopped onion

3 tablespoons apple cider vinegar
1/4 cup safflower oil
1/4 cup mellow white miso
1/4 cup fresh minced parsley

In a small pot, cook the tofu 1 minute in boiling water. Rinse in cold water, and drain. In a blender, process the tofu, avocado, garlic, onion, vinegar, oil, miso, half the parsley, and 1/2 cup of water until smooth. Pour into a bowl and stir in the remaining parsley. Chill slightly before serving.

Creamy Walnut-Miso Dressing

MAKES 1 CUP

Think of this as an Asian pesto, made with miso and onions instead of the Parmesan cheese and garlic used in a traditional pesto. This dressing goes as well on pasta or steamed green beans as it does on green salads.

$^1/_3$ *cup walnuts*
$^1/_4$ *cup walnut oil, or sesame oil*
2 *tablespoons mellow white miso*
2 *tablespoons chopped onion*

1 *tablespoon rice syrup*
$2^1/_2$ *tablespoons brown rice vinegar*
Pinch white pepper

In a dry skillet over medium heat, toss the walnuts until fragrant, 5–10 minutes. Stir continuously so they don't burn.

In a food processor, process all the ingredients until smooth. Chill the dressing. If it is too thick, thin with water back to its original consistency.

Charmoula Vinaigrette

This aromatic dressing is one reason so many people fall in love with Moroccan food. Use as a sauce on poached or broiled fish, as well as tossed with romaine lettuce, or over steamed vegetables.

$1/2$ cup fresh lemon juice

3 cloves garlic, very finely minced

1-inch-piece ginger, peeled and finely minced

1 teaspoon paprika

$1/2$ teaspoon cayenne pepper

2 teaspoons ground toasted cumin seeds

$1/2$ cup chopped fresh parsley

$1/2$ cup chopped cilantro

1 cup extra virgin olive oil

$1/2$ teaspoon sea salt

$1/4$ teaspoon freshly ground black pepper

In a medium bowl, mix the lemon juice, garlic, ginger, paprika, cayenne, and cumin. Whisk in the parsley, cilantro, and oil. Season to taste with salt and pepper.

Sweet Basil Dressing

Everyone loves the aromatic flavor of basil, and it also happens to be a good source of vitamins A and C. Try this dressing brushed on fresh corn, blended into mashed potatoes, or over broiled sole and scrod.

1 cup coarsely chopped basil leaves
3 tablespoons plus 2 teaspoons lemon juice
1 clove garlic, minced
2 teaspoons rice syrup

¼ teaspoon sea salt
⅛ teaspoon freshly ground pepper
⅔ cup extra virgin olive oil

Combine all the ingredients in a blender. Add 3 tablespoons water and blend until creamy. Pour into a cruet or jar, cap tightly, and refrigerate. Keeps several weeks.

Oregano Croutons

These savory croutons provide just the right crunch to green salads while adding hardly any fat. Since they are made using olive oil, the little fat in them is rich in beneficial monounsaturates. Whole-wheat bread gives them a particularly nutty flavor.

1 tablespoon extra virgin olive oil
1/2 teaspoon sea salt
1/4 teaspoon dried oregano
1/4 teaspoon dried sage

1/4 teaspoon dried thyme
1 tablespoon minced garlic
2 cups cubed whole-wheat sourdough bread (cut into 1/2-inch cubes)

Preheat oven to 350 degrees. In a large bowl, combine the oil, salt, oregano, sage, thyme, and garlic. Add the bread cubes and toss in mixture to coat thoroughly.

Spread seasoned bread cubes on a baking sheet in one layer. Bake 20 minutes, or until croutons are just crisp. Croutons keep 3–4 days in a tightly sealed container.

9. Sauces

 Making interesting meals, spending a modest amount of time in the kitchen, and consuming fewer dairy products and less wheat are the most difficult challenges our readers say they encounter when following a vegetarian or vegan diet. A repertoire of the right sauce recipes is one way we help them deal with these problems.

Many of the sauces offered in *Natural Health* can be made quickly and used to add different personalities to a plate of steamed vegetables, cooked grains, and beans. If you develop a collection of these flavorful sauces and marinades, it becomes easy to serve up simple food several times a week without boring your family.

Many vegetarians find that dairy-based white sauces and flour-thickened gravies are familiar, convenient ways to add satisfaction to a meal. Along with our readers, we believe that there is a place on the table for these rich sauces, if enjoyed in moderation. Over time, though, our readers have asked for other ways to liven up a meal—and for good-tasting ways to make these traditional sauces when they don't want to use dairy products, other animal foods, or wheat flour.

The recipes in this chapter reflect a variety of dietary interests. Some show you how to make classic sauces like flour-thickened white sauce, creamy mushroom sauce, and rich gravy by replacing traditional ingredients with those suited to a whole-foods, vegetarian, or vegan diet. Other recipes, like Scallion Butter (page 161) and Three-Pepper Relish (page 176), take a more free-handed approach. You'll find ingredients in these sauces that may be new to you. These are foods chosen because they add exciting, vibrant flavor or help you get good-textured sauces. You will also find sauces here with clear ethnic roots, mostly from Asia.

Much as they add interest to dishes, many sauces are also loaded with unwanted calories and fat or other nutrients you don't want. Our recipes take a different approach. Each of these sauces adds positive nutritional value, from the vitamin A in Cilantro Sauce (page 173) to the iron and calcium in sauces made with tahini, to the vitamin C in Tropical Miso Sauce (page 170). In fact, they can help you enjoy a more complete diet. For example, if you do not eat dairy products, sauces made with tahini or soy milk offer necessary calcium, while Fresh Mint Chutney (page 175) provides stomach-soothing benefits that make digesting a spicy Indian curry easier.

Sauces are created to accompany dishes. They complement other foods, either by enhancing the flavors in a dish or by adding contrast. Each sauce becomes the perfect embellishment when served with the right partner. To help you find appropriate combinations, along with every sauce recipe we offer suggestions for using it. Once you try a sauce, though, you'll probably find a variety of ways to use it with dishes you already serve.

Scallion Butter

Try this creamy spread on corn bread. It also goes nicely on a baked potato. The tahini and scallions supply the calcium and vitamin A you would get from dairy butter, without the cholesterol. In addition, scallions are a source of folic acid and iron.

2 bunches scallions, trimmed
1/2 teaspoon Ginger Juice (page 241)
1 tablespoon umeboshi paste

2 tablespoons chopped fresh parsley
2 tablespoons tahini
1 tablespoon fresh lemon juice

In a large pot of boiling water, blanch scallions 30 seconds. Drain, cool slightly, and chop into large pieces. Place the scallions in a blender and puree. Add the ginger juice to the blender with the *unemboshi* paste, parsley, tahini, and lemon juice, and blend until the mixture is the consistency of thick cream. Scrape into a bowl, cover, and refrigerate. When chilled, the mixture will set like butter. Refrigerated, it will keep 2–3 days.

Honeyed Teriyaki Sauce

Teriyaki sauce adds wonderful flavor to baked salmon and grilled foods. Unfortunately, commercially made varieties are basically flavored sugar syrup. This recipe re-creates the satisfying flavor of a classic teriyaki sauce without the refined sugar or artificial flavorings.

$^1/_3$ *cup sake*
$^1/_3$ *cup* mirin
$^1/_3$ *cup natural soy sauce*

2 teaspoons honey
$^1/_4$ *teaspoon ground ginger*

In a small saucepan over medium heat, mix together the sake, *mirin,* soy sauce, and honey. Stir to blend. Bring mixture to a boil. Reduce the heat and mix in the ground ginger. Simmer until the honey is dissolved. Use immediately, or cool, pour into a jar, and refrigerate. Keeps 2–3 weeks.

Tofu Sour Cream

Sour cream is loaded with saturated fat and cholesterol. This low-fat version tastes almost like the real thing, and does not contain the vegetable gums and gelatin used to thicken most low-fat dairy sour cream. Replace the olive oil with canola oil if you plan to use this sauce on fruits or with desserts.

8 ounces soft tofu
1 tablespoon extra virgin olive oil
1 tablespoon brown rice vinegar

1 tablespoon fresh lemon juice
Pinch sea salt
Pinch ground coriander

In a medium saucepan, bring 1 quart of water to a boil and drop in the tofu. Just after the water returns to a boil, remove the tofu and drain. Place the tofu in a blender with ¼ cup of water and add the oil, vinegar, lemon juice, salt, and coriander. Puree until creamy. Keeps, refrigerated, 2–3 days.

Heavenly Horseradish Sauce

Horseradish is traditionally served with fish and boiled beef. A cruciferous vegetable, this gnarled root may have cancer-preventing properties. Try adding a dollop of this pungent sauce to tuna and potato salads.

3-inch-piece horseradish root
¼ *cups chopped scallions, white part only*
¼ *cup extra virgin olive oil*
¼ *cup* mirin
¼ *cup brown rice vinegar*
¼ *cup mayonnaise*

Pinch sea salt
Pinch black pepper
2 cloves garlic, minced
1 tablespoon prepared mustard
2 tablespoons minced fresh parsley

Peel and grate the horseradish root on the small holes of a grater. (Fresh horseradish is notoriously strong; if you get your face too close to the grater your eyes will water profusely.)

In a blender, combine the horseradish, scallions, and olive oil, and puree for 1 minute. Add the *mirin,* vinegar, mayonnaise, salt, pepper, garlic, mustard, and parsley. Puree until smooth and creamy. Adjust seasonings to taste. Refrigerated, this sauce will keep for several days.

NOTE: You can use ¼ cup bottled horseradish, which is preserved with vinegar. If you use the bottled variety, reduce the quantity of rice vinegar to 2 tablespoons.

Sweet and Sour Sauce

Most commercially made versions of this Asian sauce contain little nutritional value beyond empty calories from refined sugar: Here, apple juice and cider vinegar provide the sweetness. Use this sauce to liven up rice, tofu dishes, and stir-fried vegetables. Pour the vegetable-studded version over rice, and you'll have a satisfying vegetarian dish.

1 cup apple juice
1/3 cup cider vinegar
1/4 cup honey
1/2 tablespoon grated fresh ginger

3 tablespoons natural soy sauce
2 tablespoons arrowroot mixed with 2 tablespoons cold water

In a saucepan, combine the apple juice, vinegar, honey, ginger, and soy sauce. Bring to a boil, then reduce to a simmer. Stir the arrowroot mixture into the simmering sauce and continue stirring until the mixture thickens.

VARIATION:

2 tablespoons sesame oil
1 onion, halved and thinly sliced
1 carrot, julienned

1 red bell pepper, cored, seeded, and julienned

In a skillet, heat the oil over medium heat, and sauté the onion, carrot, and pepper until soft, about 5 minutes. Stir the cooked vegetables into the simmering apple juice mixture and simmer about 5 minutes before adding the arrowroot.

Hearty Gravy

Nutritional yeast, which is commonly known as brewer's yeast and is high in B vitamins is one of the most useful flavor enhancers in the vegetarian pantry. Look for it in natural food stores. This sauce goes especially well with millet and buckwheat.

1½ tablespoons extra virgin olive oil
  1 cup diced onion (1 medium onion)
  2 cloves garlic, minced
  3 tablespoons whole-wheat flour
  2 tablespoons nutritional yeast
1²/3 cups Basic Vegetable Stock (page 21)

3 tablespoons barley miso
¼ teaspoon dried basil
   Several sprigs parsley, chopped
1 tablespoon mirin
1 tablespoon arrowroot dissolved in
   1 tablespoon water (optional)

In a medium skillet, heat the oil. Add the onion and garlic, and sauté over medium heat 3–4 minutes, until softened. Reduce the heat and add the flour and yeast. Cook, stirring constantly, until the flour is lightly browned, about 3 minutes. Slowly pour in 1½ cups of the stock while stirring briskly to keep the flour from lumping. Stir constantly until gravy begins to simmer and thicken.

In a small bowl, combine the miso with the remaining stock and add to the pan along with the basil, parsley, and *mirin*. Simmer gently, uncovered, for about 15 minutes, stirring occasionally.

Keep warm until served. If the gravy gets too thick, add a little more stock; if it gets too thin, cook down to the desired consistency or slowly stir in the arrowroot mixture.

White Sauce

A longtime classic, white sauce is usually made with milk. This recipe shows how you can replace the milk with soy beverage when you do not wish to use dairy foods. When you want a cheese sauce, stir a cup of shredded soy cheese—or regular cheese—into the hot sauce, plus a dash of cayenne pepper. Stir until the cheese melts. Use white sauce on vegetables and when making lasagna.

1 tablespoon butter or margarine
1/2 cup minced onion
1 1/4 teaspoons sea salt
1/4 teaspoon nutmeg

1/4 teaspoon freshly ground black pepper
1 1/4 cups plain soy beverage
3 tablespoons unbleached white flour

In a saucepan, melt the butter or margarine, add the onion and salt, and sauté 2–3 minutes. Add the nutmeg, pepper, and soy beverage, and 3/4 cup of water. Bring to a boil slowly to avoid scorching the soy beverage.

In a small bowl, add just enough cold water to the flour to make a paste with the consistency of heavy cream. Stir until smooth. Slowly add 1/2 cup of the hot sauce to the flour and water, stirring continuously to avoid lumping. Pour the flour mixture into the saucepan. Stir well and simmer, stirring the mixture occasionally, until the flour is cooked and the sauce has thickened, 8–10 minutes.

Miso Ginger Noodle Sauce

MAKES 1 CUP

Miso and tahini blend together to make this Asian-inspired noodle sauce. Use it on soba or spaghetti and serve hot or at room temperature, topped with chopped scallions and fresh cilantro.

4 tablespoons mellow barley miso
4 tablespoons tahini
2 tablespoons fresh lemon juice
1 tablespoon mirin

1 teaspoon grated ginger
1 clove garlic, minced
  Pinch dried tarragon

In a saucepan, combine the miso and tahini. Gradually stir in ½ cup water, a little at a time, mixing well to form a smooth sauce. Add the lemon juice, *mirin,* ginger, garlic, and tarragon, and bring just to a simmer. If it is too thick, add a little more water; if too thin, simmer briefly to thicken. This sauce keeps 2–3 days in a sealed container in refrigerator, but is best when used the day it is made.

Creamy Vegetable Pasta Sauce

You don't need to avoid white sauces if you stick with this satisfying low-fat version. It's a gift for vegans and anyone else who needs to avoid dairy foods. Use a well-flavored stock to make this sauce. Serve it over pasta, with seitan, and on brown rice.

1½ tablespoons canola oil
½ cup minced onion
1 cup sliced mushrooms
Pinch plus ½ teaspoon sea salt
2 tablespoons arrowroot
¾ cup plain soy beverage

1 cup Basic Vegetable Stock (page 21)
1 bay leaf
Dash white pepper
¼ onion studded with 2 whole cloves
1 tablespoon mirin
Pinch dried marjoram

In a medium skillet, heat the oil and sauté the onion over medium heat until translucent, about 5 minutes. Add the mushrooms and pinch of salt, and sauté briefly. Add the arrowroot and sauté over low heat 1–2 minutes.

In a small bowl, combine the soy beverage and stock, and slowly add to the pan while stirring briskly until the sauce thickens. Add the bay leaf, ½ tablespoon salt, pepper, onion, *mirin,* and marjoram. Simmer gently 15–20 minutes. Adjust seasonings to taste. Remove bay leaf before serving.

Tropical Miso Sauce

This simple sauce is wonderful on steamed vegetables, particularly dark greens. The orange juice contains vitamin C that helps your body absorb the iron in the tahini and the greens. If you like, whip some silken tofu into this sauce and use it as a dip for raw vegetables.

2 tablespoons mellow white miso
5 tablespoons orange juice

2 teaspoons tahini
1 tablespoon chopped chives

In a small bowl, mix all the ingredients to a consistency resembling thick cream. Pour over vegetables just before serving.

Mustard Cayenne Sauce

This pungent sauce is great on baked potatoes or served as a dip for chips. *Umeboshi* (a pickled sour Japanese plum) and cayenne pepper are known for their ability to stimulate digestion and ease discomfort from overeating. Take advantage of these benefits by serving this sauce as a dip at parties.

1 *tablespoon tahini*
2 *tablespoons mustard seeds, coarsely ground*
2 *teaspoons* umeboshi *paste*

1 *tablespoon fresh lemon juice*
    Pinch cayenne pepper, or to taste
¼ *cup minced scallion, green part only*

In a blender, combine the tahini, mustard seeds, *umeboshi* paste, lemon juice, and cayenne with ¼ cup of water, and blend until creamy. Add the scallions and blend for a few seconds more, until the dressing is not lumpy and can be poured easily over a salad. Don't overmix, or you'll lose the contrast between the mustard base and the green scallions. Refrigerated in a covered jar, the sauce keeps for several weeks.

Parsley Pepper Poaching Sauce

Fish, tempeh, and tofu pick up a lively Italian flavor when baked or braised in this sauce. It's a perfect example of how you can add extra nutrients to a meal through well-chosen seasonings.

3 tablespoons brown rice vinegar
5 tablespoons extra virgin olive oil
1 tablespoon fresh lemon juice
1/4 cup chopped fresh parsley
2 heaping tablespoons minced green
   bell pepper
2 heaping tablespoons minced carrot

Pinch cayenne pepper
Pinch paprika
1/4 teaspoon dried basil
1/4 teaspoon dried tarragon
1/4 teaspoon dried oregano
1/4 teaspoon sea salt

Place all the ingredients in a food processor, crushing the basil, tarragon, and oregano between your fingers as you add them. Blend until sauce is smooth.

Store in a tightly covered jar. Refrigerated, this sauce keeps for several months.

Cilantro Sauce

The pungency of fresh coriander or cilantro helps give many Mexican, Chinese, and Indian dishes their distinctive flavors. Using it adds extra vitamins A and C to dishes. It is also helpful for soothing stomachaches. Spread this sauce on bread or serve it over warm pasta.

1 bunch fresh cilantro
2 cloves garlic
¼ teaspoon sea salt

1 teaspoon tahini
1 tablespoon fresh lemon juice

Place the cilantro and garlic in a food processor and process to a paste. Add the salt, tahini, and lemon juice, and blend briefly.

Jalapeño Onion Chutney

Indian chutneys can be blends of fresh ingredients or cooked sauces. This fiery chutney made with fresh ingredients keeps several days in the refrigerator. Serve with Vegetable Chick-pea Fritters with Ginger Dip (page 119) or corn chips.

*1 small fresh jalapeño pepper, seeded
  (wear rubber gloves) or 1 tablespoon
  canned jalapeño peppers
½ small tomato, seeded and chopped*

*1 tablespoon fresh lemon juice
1 teaspoon sea salt
1½ cups grated onion*

In a blender, puree the pepper, tomato, lemon juice, and salt. Pour into a bowl and add the onion. Mix well. Refrigerated, this sauce will keep several days.

Fresh Mint Chutney

This Indian sauce tastes sweet, sour, hot, and minty all at once. Serve it on steamed vegetables. It is also good blended into cooked rice or millet. Mint is a good tonic for the nerves. It is also used in herbal medicine to allay colds. Look for tamarind and mustard oil at Indian food stores.

4 cups loosely packed fresh mint leaves
1–2 fresh green chilies, seeded and chopped (wear rubber gloves), or 1–2 tablespoons chopped canned chilies

2 tablespoons tamarind pulp
1 tablespoon mustard oil
2 tablespoons Sucanat

In a medium pot, bring 1 quart of water to a boil. Add the mint leaves and cook just until they wilt, 1–2 minutes. Drain the leaves well in a colander and place them in a food processor with the chilies, tamarind, mustard oil, and Sucanat. Process until well pureed.

Refrigerated, the chutney keeps a week. The pulp and liquid will separate, so stir before serving.

Three-Pepper Relish

This sauce is made with sweet bell peppers and just enough hot pepper sauce to give it a kick. Bell peppers are among the richest sources of vitamin C. The red ones are also rich in beta carotene. Serve with cooked beans, rice, or grilled tempeh.

2 tablespoons extra virgin olive oil
1 red bell pepper, seeded and diced
1 yellow bell pepper, seeded and diced
1 green bell pepper, seeded and diced
1 large red onion, diced

1 tablespoon bottled hot sauce, or to taste
1 tablespoon mirin
2 tablespoons white miso
1 teaspoon kuzu dissolved in 2 tablespoons water

In an iron skillet, heat the oil and sauté peppers and onion over medium heat until tender, 8–10 minutes. Add hot sauce. Add the *mirin*.

Dissolve the miso in a few tablespoons of water and add to the peppers. Cook 2–3 minutes, and add the dissolved *kuzu*. Cook, stirring constantly, until sauce boils and turns translucent. Serve immediately.

10. Breakfasts and Brunches

When you want to improve your diet, breakfast is the easiest place to start. It's the meal where whole grains and other natural foods rich in complex carbohydrates, protein, fiber, vitamins, and minerals fit right in. So why don't more people take advantage of this? Because they dislike the tastes and textures of many of these foods.

So we've spent lots of time exploring how to get beyond the "ugh" reaction to whole-wheat pancakes, hot oatmeal, toasted multigrain bread, and other whole breakfast foods. Our goal is to help you think creatively about ways to enjoy a healthful meal in the morning, leaving out the excess, empty calories from fat and refined foods. For example, spread spiced, creamed honey on those pancakes; sprinkle what you like best on that oatmeal, whether it's maple syrup and a modest pat of butter, or a tablespoon of cocoa powder mixed with Sucanat, an unrefined sweetener made from sugarcane juice that blends particularly well with chocolate flavors; top your whole-grain toast with peanut butter and juice-sweetened fruit spread, or mashed banana and slices of preservative-free bacon; even enjoy a poached egg nestled on a bed of our oven-baked hash browns. Breakfast is such an important meal that it's worth a bit of compromise to start the day with a good foundation. As we've said before, moderation is the key.

Since many readers said muffins and other baked goods, old-fashioned pancakes, and waffles would most tempt them not to skip breakfast, we've spent lots of time developing recipes for them. You'll see that, with the judicious use of eggs and either milk or soy beverage, these recipes produce a variety of breakfast and brunch favorites that taste like treats.

The base for many of these recipes is a mix of dry ingredients you can put together in large batches and store in your refrigerator. When you want to make waffles, a streusel-topped coffee cake, or some muffins, just scoop out the amount called for in the recipe, add the other ingredients to it, mix, and bake or pour it into your waffle iron.

Since we like foods that taste the way nature created them, we take a measured approach to using one ingredient in place of another. In baking, we have found that using soy beverage in place of milk does affect the results. Still, vegans and others who avoid using dairy products will be satisfied with the results they get with these recipes. We also think the scrambled tofu and tempeh sausage will pleasantly surprise anyone who tries them.

When you have time to relax over brunch, think about including fresh fruits on the menu in addition to juice. While juice can provide useful vitamins and minerals, it does not contain the fiber found in whole fruits. Also, fruit salad or a colorful fruit platter offers the chance to serve an assortment of fruits from the five fruit families: melons, citrus, berries, stone fruits, and apples and pears. This is important because variety is the key to reaping the nutritional advantages of fresh fruits. To give you an idea, oranges and grapefruits are high in vitamin C, while apples and pears are good sources of soluble fiber, and bananas are rich in potassium but contain little dietary fiber.

Breakfast and brunch are also easy times to fit nuts and seeds into a meal, rather than just using them for snacks. Along with mixing chopped nuts or a measure of seeds into muffins, try adding them to pancakes or sprinkling them on cereals. We are particularly fond of toasted sesame seeds on oatmeal.

Nuts and seeds contain 8 to 20 percent protein, and some, like almonds, filberts, sesame seeds, and Brazil nuts, provide helpful amounts of calcium. Many people avoid seeds and nuts because they are high in fat, but most of their fat is unsaturated. A hefty percentage is monounsaturated fat, which lowers harmful LDL cholesterol and raises helpful HDL cholesterol. The exception is coconut, which contains primarily saturated fat.

Oil-rich seeds and nuts are also a rich source of vitamin E. Like vitamin C and beta carotene, vitamin E is a powerful antioxidant. It gathers up free radicals, which are unstable molecules that have been linked to the formation of cancer, heart disease, and various chronic disorders. Vitamin E helps retard cellular aging and speeds the healing of wounds. And if you worry about children who are constantly eating peanut butter, keep in mind these nuts are a good source of choline, a chemical that enhances memory, and of vitamin B_6. If you are concerned about the high fat content in nuts and seeds, just limit the amount you eat to a handful or two tablespoons of nut butters a day.

Basic Breakfast Baking Mix

This basic recipe is the foundation for muffins, pancakes, waffles, biscuits, and scones. Use it in the recipes that follow. It can also be used to replace the refined white flour and other dry ingredients in your favorite breakfast recipes. The oils in whole grains oxidize rapidly, so mix up only as much of this blend as you'll use in a few weeks, and keep it in an airtight container in the refrigerator.

1 cup whole-wheat flour
$^1/_2$ cup whole-wheat pastry flour
$^1/_2$ cup unbleached white flour
$^1/_2$ teaspoon sea salt

$^1/_2$ teaspoon baking soda
2 teaspoons nonaluminum baking powder
$1^1/_4$ teaspoons cinnamon

Into a bowl, sift together all ingredients and mix well. Refrigerate in a tightly covered container.

Egg-free Pancakes

These pancakes cook up light and tender without eggs or a packaged egg substitute. Whether you use cow's milk or soy beverage, you'll get calcium, but the soy beverage lets you avoid saturated fats and cholesterol. A tablespoon of toasted sesame seeds mixed into the batter adds calcium and gives these pancakes extra flavor.

1 tablespoon canola oil
1 tablespoon maple syrup
1 cup plain soy beverage, or skim milk

2 cups Basic Breakfast Baking Mix
(page 180)

In a bowl, combine the oil and maple syrup. Mix in the soy beverage and 1 cup of water. Fold in the basic mix with a few light strokes. The batter should be thin enough to pour in an even stream, but not watery. If it seems too thin, add more basic mix; if too thick, add a little water.

Heat a very lightly oiled skillet or griddle until drops of cold water dance on the surface before evaporating. If the water vanishes immediately, the pan is too hot. For each pancake, pour ¼ cup of batter from a measuring cup. Cook until bubbles appear on the upper surface, and turn before the bubbles break. Brown the second side. If the center is doughy, the pan was probably too hot. Brush the pan lightly with oil between bakings. Serve hot with maple syrup or apple butter.

VARIATION: Just before cooking, fold into the batter 1 cup of blueberries or 1 cup of thinly sliced apples, peaches, or strawberries.

Old-fashioned Waffles

Waffles can be a high-fat, high-cholesterol nightmare. Here, we've kept one egg but replaced the butter and milk with cholesterol-free oil and soy beverage. Top these waffles with sliced fresh strawberries or Ginger Peach Compote (page 235), or serve with warm maple syrup, or apple butter.

3 tablespoons canola oil
1 egg, beaten
1 cup plain soy beverage, or skim milk

2 cups Basic Breakfast Baking Mix (page 180)

In a bowl, combine the oil, egg, soy beverage or milk, and 1 cup of water. Blend in the basic mix just until it is moistened. The batter should be thin enough to pour evenly, but not watery. It will thicken as it sits. If it becomes too thick, add a little more water.

Oil and heat a waffle iron. Cook waffles according to manufacturer's directions. Brush iron lightly with oil between waffles.

Raisin Drop Biscuits

Most biscuits are made with vegetable shortening, which consists of hydrogenated vegetable oils. Hydrogenation is a process that pumps hydrogen gas through normally unsaturated vegetable oils. It converts such oils into saturated fats. In place of shortening, we use canola oil to lighten these biscuits. Serve them right from the oven, accompanied by creamed honey and apple butter.

2 cups Basic Breakfast Baking Mix
  (page 180)
¹/₄ cup canola oil

¹/₄ cup rice syrup
¹/₄ cup plain soy beverage, or skim milk
¹/₂ cup raisins

Preheat oven to 425 degrees.

Place the basic mix in a medium bowl, and make a well in the center. Pour the oil into the well. With a fork, quickly and lightly incorporate the dry mix into the oil until the mixture resembles coarse meal.

In a small bowl, whisk together the syrup, soy beverage, and 3 tablespoons of water. Add the raisins. Add the wet ingredients to the flour mixture, stirring with a fork just until a dough is formed. Onto an ungreased baking sheet, drop the dough in 3-inch mounds, 2 inches apart. Bake 10 minutes, then lower the heat to 350 degrees and bake 8–10 minutes more, or until the biscuits are golden. Serve immediately.

Blueberry Coffee Cake

Feel good when you serve this whole-grain coffee cake at breakfast. It's too good to limit to the morning, so have it as an afternoon snack, too. This cake freezes well; bake up two at a time and save a second cake to serve another day.

STREUSEL TOPPING
1 tablespoon canola oil
3/4 cup chopped walnuts
2 tablespoons rice syrup

1 tablespoon whole-wheat pastry flour
1 teaspoon cinnamon

CAKE
1/4 cup canola oil
3/4 cup rice syrup
1 teaspoon vanilla
1 egg, beaten

2 cups Basic Breakfast Baking Mix (page 180)
1 cup blueberries

Preheat oven to 350 degrees. Oil a 9 × 9-inch baking pan.

For topping: In a small skillet, heat the oil over medium heat and sauté the nuts until they are fragrant, 5–7 minutes. Remove the pan from heat and stir in syrup, flour, and cinnamon.

For cake: In a large bowl, combine well the oil, rice syrup, vanilla, and egg with 3/4 cup of water. Fold in the basic mix, just until it is moistened, then fold in the blueberries with as few strokes as possible. The batter should be thin enough to pour evenly. If it is too thick, add a little more water.

Pour the batter into the prepared pan, and sprinkle the streusel topping evenly over the batter. Bake 30–40 minutes. When the cake is done, it should pull away from the sides of the pan and spring back when the top is pressed, and a tester inserted into the center should come out clean.

Cool on a wire rack; serve warm or at room temperature.

Apricot Bran Muffins

Dried apricots are concentrated little nuggets of nutrients. They're high in vitamin A, beta-carotene, iron, and niacin. Look for unsulfured dried Turkish apricots at natural food stores. Unsulfured dried fruits usually look darker than ones treated with sulfites, which are added to keep them from turning brown. We find Turkish dried apricots are particularly sweet. Save a few of these hearty muffins to toast and enjoy with afternoon tea.

2 cups Basic Breakfast Baking Mix
   (page 180)
1 cup wheat bran
³/₄ cup chopped dried apricots
¹/₄ cup canola oil

²/₃ cup rice syrup
¹/₂ teaspoon orange extract, or 2 teaspoons
   grated orange zest
1 egg, beaten
1¹/₂ cups apricot juice

Preheat oven to 400 degrees. Oil a 12-cup muffin tin.

In a medium bowl, mix together the basic mix and wheat bran. Add the apricots. In another bowl, whisk together the oil and syrup, then add the orange extract or zest and egg and beat well. Mix in the juice. Fold together the wet and dry ingredients, just until all the flour mixture is moistened.

Spoon into the muffin tin, nearly filling the cups. Bake 20 minutes, or until the tops spring back when lightly touched and a tester inserted in the center comes out clean.

Cool on a wire rack 10–15 minutes, then carefully remove muffins.

Carrot Breakfast Muffins

Carrots are the number-one dietary source for beta carotene, a nutrient whose antioxidant properties may help reduce the risk of cancer. Pairing shredded carrots with raisins gives these muffins appealing sweetness along with extra fiber. Serve them with cream cheese and orange marmalade.

½ teaspoon ground ginger	1 egg, beaten
2 cups Basic Breakfast Baking Mix (page 180)	1 cup finely grated carrot
¼ cup canola oil	¼ cup raisins
⅔ cup rice syrup	¾ cup apple juice

Preheat oven to 400 degrees. Oil a 12-cup muffin tin.

In a large bowl, mix the ginger into the basic mix. In another bowl, whisk together the oil and syrup. Mix in the egg, then add the carrot, raisins, and juice. Fold the dry and wet ingredients together, just until the flour mixture is moistened.

Spoon the batter into the muffin cups to about three-quarters full. Bake 20 minutes, or until the tops spring back when lightly touched and a tester inserted in the center comes out clean.

Cool on a wire rack 5–10 minutes before carefully removing muffins.

Sweet Potato Muffins

If you like sweet potato pie, you'll love these moist, nut-studded muffins. Sweet potatoes are a good source of dietary fiber, beta carotene, vitamins, and minerals. Mashed canned yams can substitute for homemade sweet potatoes. If you use canned yams, it may be necessary to reduce the amount of liquid because of the moisture in the yams.

2 cups Basic Breakfast Baking Mix (page 180)
$1/2$ teaspoon cinnamon
$1/2$ teaspoon freshly grated nutmeg
1 egg, beaten

$3/4$ cup cooked sweet potato puree
$1/3$ cup corn oil
$3/4$ cup plain soy beverage, or skim milk
$1/2$ cup chopped walnuts

Preheat oven to 400 degrees. Oil a 12-cup muffin tin.

In a large bowl, whisk together the basic mix, cinnamon, and nutmeg. In a medium bowl, combine the egg, sweet potato, oil, and soy beverage or milk. Make a well in the center of the dry ingredients, and pour in the wet ingredients and add the nuts. Mix just enough to moisten.

Fill the muffin cups two-thirds full and bake for about 25 minutes, or until a cake tester inserted in the center comes out clean. Serve hot with apple butter or berry jam.

Banana Oat Pancakes

Here's a truly delicious way to eat your oat bran. Oat bran is high in soluble fiber, which, studies have shown, can help reduce blood cholesterol levels. In addition, oats provide more protein than wheat. Potassium-rich bananas add natural sweetness to these pancakes. This recipe uses Sucanat, an evaporated sugarcane sweetener, which you can find in natural food stores. Serve topped with warm maple syrup.

1 cup rolled oats, ground into a coarse meal in a blender or food processor
1/2 cup whole-wheat pastry flour
1/2 cup unbleached white flour
2 teaspoons baking soda
1 tablespoon Sucanat
1 very ripe banana, mashed (about 1/2 cup)
2 teaspoons vanilla
1 1/2 cups plain yogurt
3 egg whites
2 tablespoons canola oil, or melted butter
1/2 cup coarsely chopped walnuts, for garnish

In a medium bowl, mix together the ground oats, flours, baking soda, and Sucanat. Stir in the banana and vanilla. Add the yogurt, stirring until well combined.

In another bowl, beat the egg whites until stiff but not dry. Using a spatula, fold the egg whites into the batter. Fold in oil or butter.

Heat a large, heavy skillet or griddle over moderate heat until a drop of water skitters on the surface. Lightly oil the skillet or griddle. For each pancake, pour 1/4 cup of the batter onto the pan, allowing room for the pancakes to spread.

Cook over moderate heat until the bubbles burst on the surface, about 1 minute. Flip the pancakes and cook until golden underneath, about 1 minute longer. Serve hot, garnished with the chopped walnuts.

Yogurt Pecan Coffee Cake

Yogurt helps make baked goods light and tender. It also adds calcium and B$_{12}$. The cinnamon and nut topping on this cake goes perfectly with a cup of coffee or peppermint herb tea.

PECAN TOPPING

1 cup finely chopped lightly toasted
  pecans
^{1}/$_3$ cup Sucanat

1 teaspoon cinnamon
4 tablespoons canola oil or melted butter

CAKE

1 cup whole-wheat pastry flour
1 cup unbleached white flour
1 teaspoon baking powder
1 teaspoon nonaluminum baking soda
^{1}/$_4$ teaspoon sea salt

^{1}/$_2$ cup maple syrup
^{1}/$_3$ cup canola oil
2 eggs, lightly beaten
1 cup plain yogurt
1 teaspoon vanilla

Preheat the oven to 350 degrees. Oil a 9-inch round or square pan.

For topping: In a small bowl, stir together the pecans, Sucanat, and cinnamon. Stir in the oil or melted butter.

For cake: In a large bowl, sift together the flours, baking powder, baking soda, and salt. In a medium bowl, beat together the maple syrup and canola oil until smooth. Beat in the eggs. Stir in the yogurt and the vanilla. Combine the wet and dry ingredients and stir just until evenly moistened.

Spread half the batter in the prepared pan, and sprinkle half the pecan topping evenly over the batter. Spread the remaining batter on top, making it as smooth as possible. Sprinkle the remaining pecan mixture evenly over the top of the batter.

Bake 40–45 minutes, or until a cake tester inserted into the center of the cake comes out clean. Cool on a wire rack 10 minutes before cutting into squares or triangles.

Wheat-free Teff Waffles

In Ethiopia, teff is used to make *injera,* a soft bread that is the main source of protein. Teff is low in gluten, so it can be tolerated by many people with wheat allergies. Teff is sold in most natural food stores. Process it in the blender to turn this pinpoint-fine grain into flour.

3/4 cups teff flour
2 teaspoons nonaluminum baking
   powder

1/4 teaspoon sea salt
3 tablespoons sesame oil
1 1/2 cups plain soy beverage

Heat a waffle iron. In a medium bowl, sift together the flour, baking powder, and salt. Make a well in the center of the sifted ingredients.

In a small bowl, combine the oil and soy beverage. Pour the wet ingredients into the well and stir with a few quick strokes, just enough to moisten the dry ingredients. The batter will have a pebbled look.

Cook in waffle iron according to manufacturer's directions.

Amasake Scones

When you want to avoid the fat and cholesterol with which most scones are loaded, try making them with *amasake,* a creamy drink made from sweet rice. It gives these scones some of the tender richness they usually get from cream or butter. Serve with your favorite fruit spread or preserves.

1/2 cup plain amasake
1/4 cup plain soy beverage
1/3 cup currants, or chopped raisins
2 teaspoons finely grated lemon zest
2 cups Basic Breakfast Baking Mix
   (page 180)

3 tablespoons corn oil
   Unbleached white flour, for rolling out dough

Preheat oven to 400 degrees. Oil two baking sheets.

In a blender, combine *amasake* and soy beverage, and process until smooth.

Pour the mixture into a small bowl and add the currants or raisins and lemon zest. Sift the baking mix into a medium bowl and mix well. Add the oil and stir briefly with a fork; then rub the mixture between your fingers until it resembles coarse sand. make a well in the center of the flour mixture. Add the *amasake* mixture and mix lightly with a fork, just until the flour is moistened evenly.

Knead the dough gently a couple of times to form a ball. The dough should be soft and slightly sticky. If it is too sticky, mix in a little flour; if it is too dry, add a bit more soy beverage or milk.

Place dough on a floured board. Sprinkle a little flour on the dough and on a rolling pin to prevent sticking. Quickly roll dough to an even 1/2-inch thickness. Cut out rounds with a biscuit cutter or glass and place them on the baking sheets.

Bake 10–15 minutes. Scones should be golden but still soft.

Western-style Scrambled Tofu

Moist and light, scrambled tofu provides the protein supplied by eggs without the cholesterol. It can also contain calcium if made using calcium sulfate or calcium chloride as the coagulant, which eggs lack. Sweet and chili peppers plus corn and a bit of Monterey Jack cheese add appealing color to this dish. Serve with whole-grain toast and Baked Confetti Hash Browns (page 194).

1 pound medium or firm tofu
2 tablespoons extra virgin olive oil
1 cup finely chopped onion
2 cloves garlic, minced
1/2 red bell pepper, cored and diced
1/2 green bell pepper, cored and diced
1 small jalapeño pepper, cored, seeded, and diced (wear rubber gloves)
3/4 cup whole-kernel fresh or frozen corn (1 medium ear)

1 tablespoon chili powder
1/2 teaspoon ground cumin
1/2 teaspoon dried oregano
    Dash bottled hot sauce
1/2 teaspoon sea salt
1/3 cup grated Monterey Jack cheese or soy cheese
1/4 cup minced fresh parsley

Press tofu, as described in Chapter 4 (page 71), letting it drain 20 minutes. Crumble tofu into small pieces.

In a large pan, heat the oil and sauté the onion and garlic until they begin to turn translucent, about 5 minutes. Add the peppers and corn and cook until just tender, about 5 minutes more. Add the chili powder, cumin, oregano, hot sauce, salt, and crumbled tofu. Cook over moderate heat until the liquid evaporates, 5–10 minutes. Stir in the cheese and parsley. Serve immediately.

Tempeh Sausage

Meaty-tasting tempeh makes a delicious sausage. The key is using the right blend of spices. A bit of flour binds the tempeh together so it can be formed into patties. Fry them up crisp just as you would conventional sausage patties. Loaded with protein, they can be served at breakfast or with mashed potatoes for a light supper.

8 ounces tempeh
2 tablespoons unbleached white flour
2 tablespoons natural soy sauce
$1/2$ teaspoon dried sage
$1/4$ teaspoon dried marjoram

$1/4$ teaspoon dried thyme
$1/4$ teaspoon cayenne pepper
$1/4$ teaspoon black pepper
2 tablespoons canola oil

Cut the tempeh into 2-inch squares and steam 20 minutes. When cool enough to handle, finely grate tempeh into a medium bowl. Add the flour, soy sauce, dried herbs, cayenne pepper, and black pepper, plus 2 tablespoons of water, and stir until well blended.

With your hands press the mix firmly together to form 2-inch patties.

In a heavy skillet, heat the oil and sauté the patties until well browned on both sides. Drain on paper towels and serve hot.

Baked Confetti Hash Browns

Finish these oven-baked potatoes under the broiler to give them some of the crustiness usually created by frying hash browns in bacon fat or butter. Vegetables add flavor, color, and lots of fiber. We like these wholesome potatoes any time of the day.

1 tablespoon olive oil
1 large leek, washed, trimmed, and cut into 1/2-inch slices
1 medium red onion, chopped into 1/2-inch pieces
3 cloves garlic, minced
2 sprigs fresh thyme, leaves only, or 1/2 teaspoon dried
2 carrots, peeled and diced
2 Russet potatoes, peeled and diced

1 medium red bell pepper, cut into 1/2-inch squares
1 medium zucchini, diced
1 medium yellow squash, diced
1 cup thickly sliced white mushrooms
1/2 cup thickly sliced shiitake mushrooms
3 tablespoons minced fresh parsley
1 teaspoon sea salt
1/2 teaspoon freshly ground pepper
1/4 cup grated soy cheese (optional)

In a large skillet, heat the oil over medium heat. Add the leeks, onion, garlic, and thyme leaves. Cook, uncovered, stirring frequently, until leeks and onions are soft and begin to brown, 6–8 minutes. Add the carrots and potatoes and 1/3 cup of water. Cover and cook until the vegetables are almost tender and the water is absorbed, about 15 minutes.

Add the red pepper, zucchini, yellow squash, and mushrooms, and continue to cook, uncovered, stirring occasionally, for about 5 minutes. Season the vegetables with the parsley, salt, and pepper, tossing gently to combine. Cook 3–5 minutes longer, shaking the pan occasionally to prevent sticking.

Heat the broiler. Turn the hash into a lightly oiled, shallow baking dish and put under the broiler until vegetables begin to brown, 3–5 minutes. If using, sprinkle with soy cheese and continue broiling until cheese melts. Serve immediately.

11. Appetizers and Small Dishes

Once upon a time, our goal was eating three square meals a day. At lunch- and dinnertime, a square meal traditionally included an appetizer, a main course, and dessert. Dietary goals have changed a lot since those days.

An appetizer is still the dish served before the main course. But it's harder finding room for it in a meal. Today we are more concerned with taking in fewer calories per day—keeping consumption of fats to 30 percent or less of daily calories and getting the bulk of these calories from complex carbohydrates, fruits, and vegetables—than in sitting down to a formal meal with clearly defined courses. Instead, we often look for light meals. When we do eat an appetizer course, we want it to add nutritionally important foods to a meal rather than simply loading on extra, unwise calories.

The first course is a perfect place for foods that don't seem to fit in anywhere else in a meal. For Americans, this often means a salad of greens and other raw vegetables. We're all for starting with a salad. But we want you to have more choices, as well.

When you want to serve an opener, here are healthful appetizer ideas flexible enough to fit an assortment of mealtime moods. Many of them can work as components for a small meal, or can switch from one part of the day to another. For example, Smoked Salmon Potato Cakes (page 203) can be the elegant opener for a dinner party, one part of a leisurely brunch, or the star of a late night supper. Curried Red Lentil Pâté (page 198) can be served as a traditional first course, be presented on its own as a small dish when you feel like grazing, or take the form of an hors d'oeuvre enjoyed with a glass of wine before the main part of a meal. There are dips you can also use to make tea sandwiches, and nibbles like Sesame Walnuts (page 208) and Garlic and Herb Bagel Chips (page 209) to eat as snacks. The recipes we offer are eclectic enough to include dishes that serve all these possibilities as well as complementing the rest of a meal.

Pakoras (Indian Chick-pea Fritters)

Soft on the inside, crispy on the outside, these fritters are delicious served with Raita (page 148). For a party, drop the batter in teaspoonfuls and reduce the cooking time accordingly. Serve on toothpicks.

1 cup chick-pea flour
1/2 cup warm water
1/2 cup finely grated onion
1/4 cup finely grated carrot
1/2 cup peeled and finely grated potato

1 teaspoon sea salt
1/4 teaspoon ground black pepper
1/2 teaspoon ground coriander
1/2 teaspoon ground cumin
Canola oil for deep-frying

Sift the flour into a large bowl. Add the water slowly while beating with a whisk or electric mixer into a thick batter. Set in a warm place for 1/2 hour to ferment slightly.

With your hands, mix the onion, carrot, potato, salt, pepper, coriander, and cumin into the batter.

Fill a wok or heavy pot with oil to a depth of 2 inches, and heat to very hot but not smoking, around 300 degrees. Flatten a tablespoon of batter into a disc and drop into the hot oil. Fry 6–7 pakoras at a time without crowding. Cook the fritters for about 5 minutes, turn, and cook until golden, 2–3 minutes more. Drain on paper towels. Serve immediately or hold pakoras in a warm oven.

Curried Red Lentil Pâté

The velvety texture of red lentils is the perfect base for this vegan dish. Vegetables and generous amounts of seasonings make this loaf colorful and provide assertive flavor.

2 tablespoons plus ½ cup bread crumbs
1 cup red lentils
2 teaspoons extra virgin olive oil
1 cup diced onion
½ carrot, diced
1 cup diced celery
1 cup diced zucchini
2 teaspoons minced garlic

2 teaspoons curry powder
½ teaspoon dried basil
½ teaspoon dried oregano
½ teaspoon dried thyme
1 teaspoon sea salt
2 teaspoons prepared mustard
3 tablespoons minced fresh parsley

Add one of the following for a richer flavor (optional):

2 tablespoons drained capers
3 tablespoons pitted and diced black olives

3 tablespoons diced pimientos, or roasted red peppers

Preheat oven to 350 degrees. Oil a 9-inch baking pan or loaf pan and coat it evenly with 2 tablespoons of the bread crumbs.

Sort the lentils on a large plate to remove any tiny stones or twigs. Rinse the lentils two or three times. Drain well and put them in a heavy medium pot. Add 2 cups of water and bring to a boil. Reduce the heat and simmer, partially covered, until the liquid is absorbed, about 20 minutes.

In a large skillet, heat the oil over medium heat. Add the onion, carrot, and celery. Sauté until partially tender, 3–4 minutes, stirring frequently. Add the zucchini, garlic, curry powder, basil, oregano, thyme, and salt. Cook 3–4 minutes longer, stirring occasionally. Add the cooked lentils, mustard, parsley, and remaining ½ cup bread crumbs. Stir to combine. If using an optional ingredient, add it and stir to mix.

Spoon the lentil mixture into the prepared pan, cover with foil or parchment paper, and bake until a knife or cake tester inserted in the center comes out clean, 25–30 minutes. Allow to cool completely before slicing.

If desired, garnish paté with sliced olives, red peppers, pimientos, sliced lemons, or chopped green herbs. Serve with pita bread, whole-grain bread, or crackers.

Tomatoes Stuffed with Savory Bread Crumbs

SERVES 4

This simplified version of scalloped tomatoes requires the flavor of the ripest tomatoes you can get. Whole-wheat bread crumbs accentuate the natural, fruity sweetness of the tomatoes. Serve with Black Pepper Tofu Steaks (page 83).

2 ripe tomatoes
2 tablespoons extra virgin olive oil

³/4 cup Savory Bread Crumbs
(page 243)

Cut tomatoes in half around their equator. Gently squeeze each half to remove the seeds. With a spoon, scrape the soft center flesh out of each half and discard.

In a skillet, heat the oil over medium heat. Add the tomatoes, cut side down. Cook, covered, 3–4 minutes. Using a spatula and fork, turn tomatoes over. Stuff each half with the bread crumb mixture. Cover pan, reduce heat to low, and cook until tomatoes are done, about 5 minutes.

Breaded Sweet Onion Slices

These slabs of sweet onion topped with crisped bread crumbs make a memorable first course. You can also serve them in place of a salad. Sweet onions like Vidalia, Maui, Walla Walla, and any of a number of varieties from Texas, are sweetest just after harvesting. Look for the variety of sweet onion that's been harvested most recently: the older they get, the more water evaporates from them, and the more they develop the same bit as conventional onions.

2 *large sweet onions (about*
  1¼ pounds)
2–3 *tablespoons extra virgin olive oil*
¼ *teaspoon sea salt*

¾ *cup Savory Bread Crumbs*
  (page 243)
  Freshly ground black pepper

Peel the onions and slice them into ½-inch rings. In a large ovenproof skillet, heat the oil over medium heat. Place the onion slices in the pan in one layer and sprinkle with the salt. Cook 3–4 minutes, until bottoms of slices start to soften.

Carefully turn the onions using a spatula, keeping the rings intact. Sprinkle bread crumbs and pepper over the onions. Cover and cook until tender, about 4 minutes. If you wish to brown the tops, put the onions under broiler for 1–2 minutes. Transfer to a serving platter or individual plates and serve hot.

"Tuna" Tempeh Spread

This piquant spread can be put together up to 3 days ahead. It is a great vegetarian alternative to tuna, rich in high-quality protein and calcium, too. Stuff it into scooped-out cherry tomatoes or spread it on bread for canapés and tea sandwiches. This spread can also be served on crackers, crisps, or mini–rice cakes, or can be used to stuff endive leaves or tart shells.

8 ounces tempeh, diced
$^1/_3$ cup mayonnaise
2 tablespoons minced onion
2 tablespoons minced celery

$^1/_4$ teaspoon sea salt
2 teaspoons prepared mustard
2 tablespoons minced fresh parsley
2 tablespoons minced fresh dill

Steam the tempeh for 20 minutes. Transfer to a bowl and immediately add 1½ tablespoons of water. Mash thoroughly while tempeh is hot. Cool to room temperature, then add the mayonnaise, onion, celery, salt, mustard, parsley, and dill. Mix well.

To serve as tea sandwiches or canapés: remove the crusts from fresh whole-grain bread and cut the slices into small rectangles or triangles. Spread a generous layer of the tempeh mixture on the bread. Top with another piece of bread or serve open-faced with a slice of olive, dill pickle, or cherry tomato, and a sprig of parsley, watercress, or dill for garnish.

Avocado Sashimi

This simple dish really demands the richness of the Hass variety of avocado, grown in California. You can identify Hass avocados by their bumpy, black-green skin. Avocados are high in monounsaturated fat and beta carotene. Dipped in soy sauce with pungent wasabi, the velvety slices of avocado will remind you of raw tuna.

1 avocado
Juice of 1 lemon

4 tablespoons natural soy sauce
1 teaspoon wasabi powder

Halve the avocado lengthwise, and remove the pit. Thinly slice each half lengthwise. Peel slices and lightly coat with lemon juice to prevent discoloration. Arrange three slices each on 4 small individual dishes.

Pour 1 tablespoon of the soy sauce into 4 small, shallow bowls. Mix the wasabi with enough water to make a paste, adding the water a few drops at a time. Place a small mound of the wasabi paste on each plate with the avocado slices.

Smoked Salmon Potato Cakes

Smoked salmon is rich in omega-3 fatty acids, which have anticlotting properties and may help protect against heart attack and high blood pressure. We think it helps make these the ultimate potato pancakes. You can make the pancakes a day ahead, refrigerate them, and cook just before serving.

3 large Idaho potatoes, peeled and cut into chunks
1 teaspoon plus 2 tablespoons extra virgin olive oil
2 scallions, trimmed and sliced thin
6 ounces smoked salmon, minced
¼ cup finely chopped fresh dill
1 tablespoon fresh lemon juice
1 tablespoon plain yogurt
½ teaspoon sea salt
¼ teaspoon freshly ground pepper

Cook the potatoes in boiling water until very tender, 15–20 minutes. Place in a colander and allow to drain thoroughly. Put them through a ricer or food mill, or mash well in a bowl. Do not use a blender or food processor; it makes them too gummy. Cover and chill 30 minutes.

In a skillet, heat 1 teaspoon of the oil and sauté the scallions until soft, about 3 minutes. Stir the scallions, smoked salmon, dill, lemon juice, yogurt, salt, and pepper into the mashed potatoes.

Form the potato mixture into patties 1½ inches wide and ½ inch thick. In a large skillet over medium-high heat, heat 1 tablespoon of the oil. Cook the patties about four at a time until lightly browned, 4–5 minutes on each side. Repeat with remaining patties, adding oil as necessary.

Herbed Marinated Mushrooms

Apple cider vinegar and soy sauce give an unexpected twist to this low-fat hors d'oeuvre. It takes only 10 minutes to make this piquant dish, but keep in mind that the mushrooms must marinate for at least 12 hours. The vinegar helps improve digestion, while the mushrooms are a delicious source of B vitamins and minerals. When making a Greek salad, try some of these mushrooms in place of pickled peppers.

1 pound small white mushrooms
1 teaspoon sea salt
1 teaspoon natural soy sauce
1/2 cup apple cider vinegar
1 clove garlic, sliced or quartered
1 bay leaf

2–3 basil leaves or pinch of dried
2–3 sprigs thyme, or pinch of dried
2–3 sprigs oregano, or pinch of dried
2 tablespoons extra virgin olive oil
Fresh parsley and strips of lemon zest, for garnish (optional)

Wash the mushrooms, removing the stems and reserving for another use. Place the caps in a heatproof bowl. In a small saucepan, bring the salt, soy sauce, vinegar, garlic, bay leaf, basil, thyme, oregano, and oil to a boil. Simmer briefly, no more than 1 minute, and pour over the mushrooms.

Cool, cover bowl, and refrigerate for at least 12 hours, tossing occasionally so mushrooms marinate evenly.

To serve, drain the mushrooms and remove the bay leaf, garlic, and fresh herbs, if using.

For an attractive presentation, place the mushrooms in a serving bowl, and garnish with parsley and a few thin strips of lemon zest. Serve with toothpicks.

Walnut-Miso Dip

If you have never cooked with miso, you will be delighted with the richly intense flavor it gives to this dip. It's delicious served with celery sticks, slices of apple, or stuffed into pitted dates. If you have any dip left over, thin it with apple juice and use as a dressing on spinach salad.

1 cup walnuts
3 tablespoons mellow white miso
    About ³/4 cup Basic Vegetable Stock
    (page 21), or water

1–2 teaspoons rice syrup
    1 sprig parsley, for garnish

In a dry skillet over medium heat, toast the walnuts, stirring continuously, until fragrant, about 10 minutes. Set aside one unbroken walnut half to use for garnish.

In a blender, combine the nuts, miso, and stock or water, and blend until smooth, about 2 minutes. The dip should be the consistency of thick cream. Mix in rice syrup to taste. Walnut-Miso Dip can be made up to 2 days ahead and kept, covered, in the refrigerator. Serve the dip in a small bowl garnished with the reserved walnut half and a sprig of parsley.

Rosy Pistachio Tofu Spread

The blend of flavors in this luscious, pale pink spread defies description. Serve it on triangles of whole-wheat toast as an hors d'oeuvre. It also makes a good filling to stuff into a pita along with sprouts and thinly sliced red onion. Few sandwiches can match the protein, vitamin C, and minerals this spread provides.

14 ounces firm tofu
1 1/2 teaspoons hot sesame oil
1 1/2 teaspoons minced garlic
2 medium-size red bell peppers, seeded and julienned
2 tablespoons mellow white miso
1 tablespoon tahini
2 tablespoons fresh lemon juice
2 teaspoons fresh lime juice

1/2 teaspoon grated lime zest
1/2 teaspoon umeboshi vinegar
1 1/2 tablespoons mayonnaise
1 1/2 tablespoons maple syrup
    Pinch freshly ground pepper
1/4 cup shelled unsalted pistachio nuts, ground to a meal in blender
1/4 cup coarsely chopped shelled unsalted pistachio nuts

In a pot of boiling water, blanch the tofu for 1 minute. Remove and wrap in a clean dry cloth, squeeze out excess water, and wrap again in another clean dry cloth. Cool.

In a skillet over medium heat, heat the oil and sauté the garlic and peppers until partially soft, about 5 minutes.

In a food processor or blender, combine the tofu, miso, tahini, lemon juice, lime juice, zest, vinegar, mayonnaise, maple syrup, and white pepper. Process until smooth, about 1 minute. Transfer to large bowl and fold in the garlic and peppers, and the ground and chopped pistachio nuts.

Tomato Olivada Crostini

In Italy, they rub a clove of garlic over slices of toasted bread then top them with a delicious spread. Here, we've put the garlic right into the topping to save you time. For the best flavor, get the ripest tomatoes you can find.

2 *pepperoncini (hot pickled peppers)*
2 *cloves garlic, peeled*
1 *tablespoon capers*
2 *tablespoons tightly packed parsley leaves*
½ *cup pitted calamata or other strongly flavored olives*

1 *pound ripe tomatoes, peeled, seeded, and finely chopped*
1 *long loaf Italian or French bread*

In a food processor, puree the pepperoncini, garlic, capers, parsley, and olives until grainy but not chunky. Transfer to a bowl and stir in the tomatoes.

Slice the bread thinly and toast or grill until golden. Spread topping on hot toast and serve.

Sesame Walnuts

You may have had these crisp, savory-sweet walnuts at a Chinese restaurant. Rich in unsaturated fats, seeds and nuts are good sources of protein and vitamin E. Sesame seeds are also rich in calcium and iron. They're perfect as hors d'oeuvres or for nibbling as a snack. You can also toss a handful of them into a vegetable stir-fry for extra crunch.

½ cup unhulled sesame seeds
3 cups walnut halves
3 tablespoons rice syrup

½ teaspoon sea salt
¼ teaspoon allspice

Preheat oven to 350 degrees. Cover a cookie sheet with waxed paper and set aside.

Spread the sesame seeds in a shallow baking dish or on a jelly roll pan. Toast in the oven, stirring every 5 minutes until golden and fragrant, 15–20 minutes. A few seeds may pop. Taste them to make sure they have a roasted, buttery flavor.

Spread the walnuts on a cookie sheet and bake until slightly darker and fragrant, 8–10 minutes. Watch carefully to prevent burning.

In a large bowl, combine the rice syrup, salt, and allspice. Add the hot walnuts, and stir to coat evenly. Sprinkle the seeds over the nuts, stir gently to mix, and then spread the mixture on the prepared cookie sheet to cool. Stored in an airtight container, these nuts keep up to 1 week.

Garlic and Herb Bagel Chips

Most bagel chips are made with white flour and loaded with fat. Here, you know you are getting the nutrition of wholesome, wholegrain bagels and a modest amount of monounsaturated oil, along with delicious flavor.

6 stale whole-wheat bagels, 4–7 days old	1/2 teaspoon white pepper
1/3 cup olive oil	2 teaspoons dried oregano
2–4 tablespoons minced garlic, to taste	2 teaspoons dried basil
	1/2 teaspoon sea salt

Preheat oven to 325 degrees.

Slice each bagel to make two half-moons. Stand each half bagel on its cut edge and, using a long sharp knife, slice as thinly as possible, making 6–10 half-circles from each half bagel.

Lay the slices on a cookie sheet, almost touching one another.

In a small bowl, mix the oil, garlic, pepper, oregano, basil, and salt. (To release more flavor, grind the dried herbs in a spice mill, or rub them between your palms before combining with the other ingredients.) With a pastry brush, lightly dab each bagel slice with the oil mixture, trying to get a few garlic pieces on each slice.

Bake until the slices look toasty, about 10 minutes. They will get crisp and crunchy as they cool. Store in a moisture-proof container for up to 3 days.

12. Desserts

We're all for chocolate mousse and ice cream. We indulge joyfully in the richest versions of them we can find, occasionally and in moderation. But like most Americans, we like eating sweets often. That particularly includes pie, cake, cookies, pudding, and fruit desserts. Happily, desserts can be delightful ways to add servings of fruit and whole grains to your daily diet.

FRUITS

Fruit is a natural choice for dessert. Besides eating fruit, berries, and melons out of hand and in salads, you can use fresh and dried fruits to make compotes, cobblers, and pies, and add them to other baked treats.

Fruits are low in calories, high in soluble fiber, and, with a few exceptions like avocados and coconuts, nearly fat-free. Soluble fiber in fruits usually takes the form of pectin, which helps lower cholesterol levels and stabilize blood sugar. A single five-ounce apple supplies 17 percent of the daily recommended fiber. Studies show that pure pectin in powdered form helps suppress artery-clogging LDL cholesterol, and that when subjects consumed pectin in the form of whole fresh apples, the cholesterol reduction was even greater. Scientists are not sure just why

211

this happens, but they suspect that the combination of elements in whole fruits is the reason.

The main contribution of fruits to our diet is vitamin C and beta carotene. The National Center for Health Statistics conducted a ten-year study of more than 11,000 American men and women, probing the relationship of diet and health. When the results were analyzed by the UCLA School of Public Health, it was found that people who consumed 300 milligrams of vitamin C per day tended to be healthier overall and actually lived longer. While the current RDA for vitamin C is 60 milligrams, the study found that there was significant protection against heart disease when vitamin C was consumed at the higher level. Large amounts of vitamin C are available in many fruits. Just three to four servings of fruits high in vitamin C, like orange juice, grapefruit juice, cantaloupe, strawberries, or kiwi, will provide 300 milligrams.

Yellow and orange fruits like cantaloupe, mangoes, peaches, and nectarines supply the most beta carotene. Just half of a two-pound cantaloupe provides 100 percent of the RDA for beta carotene and vitamin C. Cantaloupes (like onions and garlic) also contain the chemical *adenosine,* which inhibits the formation of blood clots that can lead to strokes. And you don't have to eat a lot of fruit to reap their nutritional benefits. Even a single apricot, weighing about an ounce, contains enough beta carotene to supply 18 percent of the RDA for vitamin A.

Dried fruits are a concentrated source of nutrients that are often overlooked. Although vitamin C is sometimes reduced as a result of the drying process, the proportion of other vitamins and minerals is substantially increased—especially copper, iron, potassium, and beta-carotene. You can eat dried fruits raw as a convenient snack or cook them into aromatic desserts like our Ginger Peach Compote (page 235), which can be eaten straight or used as a topping for other dishes. Dried fruits are also concentrated sources of soluble fiber. Prunes are perhaps the most notable example. Prunes contain more dietary fiber than dried beans and most other fruits and vegetables.

Potassium is one of the major nutrients supplied by fresh fruits. A mineral that is lost during physical activity, it is vital to control the body's fluid balance. It also works to regulate heartbeat and blood pressure, and in older people may help to reduce the risk of stroke. Bananas supply more potassium by weight than most other fruits, but berries are also good sources.

Speaking of berries, they have their own special nutritional advantages. Cranberries, strawberries, and raspberries contain *ellagic acid,* a natural substance that research indicates helps protect against certain types of cancer. Cranberry juice also has a long history as a folk remedy for bladder and urinary tract infections. Recent studies show that it is effective not so much because of its antibiotic properties as because of its ability to prevent bacteria from sticking to the walls of the bladder and urinary tract. Other berries, like strawberries, have been shown to block cancer-causing nitrosamines in the intestines. Unfortunately, one drawback to using berries regularly is that they have a short season and are among the most perishable fruits. But studies show that frozen berries retain their nutrients for up to a year.

Some fruits, like pineapple and papaya, contain *bromelin,* an enzyme that breaks down protein. It makes these fruits useful in marinades that can help tenderize tough cuts of meat and poultry. Such fruits are excellent ways to end a heavy meal because bromelin is a powerful digestive aid.

The key to reaping the nutritional advantages of fresh fruits is to eat a wide variety. For example, apple juice contains almost no vitamin C, unless it is added during processing. But orange and grapefruit juices are high in vitamin C. Apples are high in soluble fiber, yet are not notable sources of potassium. Bananas, on the other hand, have excellent potassium, but little dietary fiber.

A good strategy is to serve fruit at every meal, including fruits of different colors and from all five fruit families: melons, citrus, berries, stone fruits, and apples and pears. Researchers from the State University of New York at Buffalo found that women who ate three cups of fruit a day had two thirds the breast cancer risk of the those who ate less than half as much fruit.

SWEETENERS

One key to wholesome desserts is avoiding the use of refined sugar, one of the leading sources of empty calories in the American diet. In the United States, sugar consumption is an incredible 120 pounds per capita per year. Not only does refined sugar provide empty calories, but metabolizing it actually drains minerals. Sugarcane, on the other hand, is rich in vitamins and minerals. The refining process during which the sugarcane juice is boiled, evaporated, and filtered to concentrate and dry it into refined sugar crystals removes all these minerals and vitamins. If you are just learning about whole foods, here is information about unrefined sweeteners you can use in place of refined sugar.

BARLEY MALT SYRUP—Made from sprouted, roasted barley. This thick, brown syrup is only about half as sweet as sugar. The complex sugars it contains enter the bloodstream gradually. This avoids the "sugar rush" caused by simple sugars. Look for it in jars in natural food stores.

BROWN RICE SYRUP—Made from brown rice and sprouted barley or barley enzymes. A thick, pale amber syrup, it is sweeter than barley malt. Like barley malt, though, rice syrup contains complex sugars to provide more even energy. Look for it in jars in natural food stores.

HONEY—Composed mainly of simple sugars, it is rich in enzymes and contains some vitamins and minerals. Raw, unfiltered honey also contains minute amounts of bee pollen. Honeys from different kinds of flowers have distinctive flavors. Experiment to find ones you like best.

MAPLE SYRUP—It takes thirty-five to forty gallons of maple sap to make a gallon of maple syrup. All grades are equal in quality and minerals; they differ only in flavor. Save money by using the stronger-flavored Grade A and Grade B Dark Amber in cooking. Maple sugar tends to cake.

MOLASSES—Made from the liquid removed from sugarcane during the refining process. It's rich in minerals but has a strong taste that limits its use in cooking mainly to gingerbread and barbecue sauces. Avoid sulfured molasses.

SORGHUM SYRUP—A thick, brown syrup made from the juice of a plant in the millet family. Fairly sweet and more mild-flavored than molasses. Used mainly in southern states.

SUCANAT—The dehydrated, granulated juice of organically grown sugarcane, this sweetener has a pronounced taste. It retains the minerals and vitamins found in sugarcane. Sucanat has a texture similar to granulated brown sugar and can be used like it.

At natural food stores, you may also find sweeteners made from fructose and from concentrated fruit juices. The main issue to keep in mind with any sweetener is whether it has been refined to the point where most of its nutrients have been removed.

Baking without refined sugar, cholesterol-rich butter, eggs, and other dairy products, and with whole-grain flour, can be challenging. We've invested a lot of time developing recipes that do this successfully. We have also focused on creating desserts that do not use wheat for those who must avoid it because of food allergies. If you are committed to following a whole-food, vegetarian, or vegan diet, we offer this collection of desserts for you to enjoy.

Maple Almond Biscotti

Biscotti are crunchy Italian cookies. They are made by baking dough once in a loaf, then slicing it and baking the sliced dough a second time. Biscotti are ideal for dipping into a steaming cup of cappuccino, a glass of sweet dessert wine, or a mug of hot cider. Made with whole-wheat flour and unrefined sweetener, they are a wholesome treat.

1 cup almonds
3 cups whole-wheat pastry flour
1 tablespoon nonaluminum baking
  powder
1/2 cup corn oil or 1/4 pound unsalted
  butter, melted

1/2 cup apple juice
1/4 cup brown rice syrup
  cup maple syrup
1 teaspoon vanilla extract
1 teaspoon almond extract
1/2 teaspoon sea salt

Preheat oven to 350 degrees. Oil a baking sheet or line it with parchment paper.

Spread the almonds on a baking sheet and toast until fragrant, 12–15 minutes. Cool and chop coarsely.

In a large bowl, combine the flour and baking powder, and stir in the almonds. In a medium bowl, combine the oil or butter, apple juice, rice syrup, maple syrup, vanilla, and almond extracts, and the salt, and mix to blend. Add this mixture to the dry ingredients and mix well. With moistened hands, form the dough into two balls. Roll out each piece of dough between sheets of waxed paper, into a strip 1/2 inch thick by 3 inches wide. (Do not make the loaf thicker or it will not bake all the way through.)

Place the dough on the baking sheet. Bake until firm and golden on the bottom, 15–20 minutes. Remove from oven and let rest until just cool enough to handle, about 3 minutes. With a sharp knife, cut each loaf of dough diagonally into 1/2–1-inch slices. Lay slices on two baking sheets. Smooth any rough edges of the cookies with your hand or a spatula. Bake until both sides are toasted, about 5–10 minutes more.

Allow to cool completely before storing in an airtight jar.

VARIATIONS: For anise biscotti, substitute 1 tablespoon anise seeds for the almonds, and omit almond extract.

For hazelnut biscotti, substitute hazelnuts for the almonds, and omit the almond extract.

For ginger-raisin biscotti, substitute for the almonds 1 teaspoon powdered ginger, ½ teaspoon ground cloves, ½ teaspoon cinnamon, and ¼ cup raisins or currants. Omit almond extract.

For Greek biscotti *(paximatha),* substitute ½ cup toasted sesame seeds for the almonds. Add 1 teaspoon cinnamon to the dry ingredients. Omit the almond extract.

Poppy Seed Cookies

MAKES 2½ DOZEN COOKIES

Oat flour makes these cookies light and crispy, and adds valuable soluble fiber, which is helpful in lowering blood cholesterol. The poppy seeds add a distinctive taste and texture.

1¼ cups rolled oats
¾ cup unbleached white flour
½ cup whole-wheat pastry flour
¼ cup poppy seeds
½ teaspoon baking soda

¼ teaspoon sea salt
½ cup maple syrup
½ cup corn oil
1 teaspoon vanilla extract
1 teaspoon rice vinegar

Preheat oven to 375 degrees. Oil a cookie sheet.

Place the oats in a food processor or blender and grind into flour. In a large bowl, combine the oats with the flours, poppy seeds, baking soda, and salt. In a medium bowl, whip together the maple syrup, corn oil, vanilla, and rice vinegar. Mix together the dry and wet ingredients. Refrigerate the dough 10 minutes.

Drop the dough by tablespoons onto the prepared cookie sheet, flattening cookies with your fingers to ½ inch thick. Bake until lightly browned, 10–12 minutes. Transfer to a wire rack to cool.

(continued on next page)

Poppy Seed Cookies (*cont.*)

VARIATION: For lemon sesame cookies, substitute ¼ cup sesame seeds, toasted in a pan over low heat until fragrant, for the poppy seeds. Add 1 tablespoon grated lemon zest to the wet ingredients.

Chewy Carrot Cookies

MAKES 3 DOZEN COOKIES

Children seem to love these moist and chewy cookies with the fresh taste of carrots. The carrots are an excellent source of vitamin A and beta carotene, while the walnuts and raisins provide a valuable source of iron, zinc, selenium, and vitamin E, which are also important for growing children.

½ cup whole-wheat pastry flour
½ cup unbleached white flour
1 teaspoon nonaluminum baking powder
¼ teaspoon sea salt
1 cup quick-cooking rolled oats
½ cup chopped roasted walnuts or
   sunflower seeds

⅓ cup raisins
2–3 carrots, shredded (about 1 cup)
½ cup maple syrup
½ cup corn oil
½ teaspoon vanilla extract

Preheat oven to 375 degrees. Oil a cookie sheet.

In a large bowl, combine the flours, baking powder, salt, and oats. Stir in the nuts or seeds, raisins, and carrots. In a bowl, whip together the maple syrup, oil, and vanilla. Stir into the flour mixture until well blended.

Using a wet teaspoon to prevent sticking, drop batter onto the prepared cookie sheet. Flatten the cookies with your fingers to ½ inch thick, and bake until golden brown, 10–12 minutes. Cool 2 minutes on the cookie sheet, and then transfer to a rack to cool completely.

Ginger Spice Cookies

Ginger lovers will adore the bite of these crisp "snaps." They are just like Grandmother's except we have left out the eggs and milk. Molasses and maple syrup add iron not found in refined sugar. Serve with your favorite flavor of ice cream or dairy-free frozen dessert.

1¼ cups unbleached white flour
 1 cup whole-wheat pastry flour
 1 teaspoon cinnamon
³/4 teaspoon ground ginger
½ teaspoon ground cloves
½ teaspoon baking soda

¼ teaspoon sea salt
½ cup corn oil
¼ cup molasses
¼ cup maple syrup
 1 teaspoon rice vinegar

In a bowl, combine the flours, cinnamon, ginger, cloves, baking soda, and salt. In another bowl, whip together the oil, molasses, maple syrup, and vinegar. Mix the wet and dry ingredients together. Wrap dough in waxed paper and refrigerate 30 minutes.

Preheat oven to 350 degrees. Oil a cookie sheet.

Drop dough by tablespoons onto the prepared cookie sheet, flattening the cookies with your fingers to ½ inch thick. Bake until lightly browned, 10–12 minutes. Transfer to a rack to cool.

Holiday Apricot Bars

The fruit filling in these delicate oat bars adds a tart sweetness. Use unsulfured apricots sold at natural food stores to make this filling. If possible, get the imported Turkish ones, which tend to be sweeter than domestically grown dried apricots.

APRICOT FILLING
1 cup dried unsulfured apricots   *¼ cup maple syrup*

DOUGH
2 cups quick-cooking rolled oats   *⅛ teaspoon ground nutmeg*
½ cup whole-wheat pastry flour   *¼ teaspoon sea salt*
½ cup unbleached white flour   *½ cup maple syrup*
1 teaspoon nonaluminum baking powder   *½ cup corn oil*
1 teaspoon cinnamon   *1 teaspoon vanilla extract*
½ teaspoon ground ginger

Preheat oven to 350 degrees. Oil a 9 × 9-inch baking pan.

For filling: In a saucepan, combine the apricots with 1 cup of water, and simmer 10 minutes, until fruit is very soft. Drain the fruit, reserving the cooking water. Puree the fruit in a blender or food processor with the maple syrup, adding as much cooking water as necessary to make a spreadable consistency.

For dough: In a large bowl, combine the oats, flours, baking powder, cinnamon, ginger, nutmeg, and salt. In another bowl, beat together the maple syrup, corn oil, and vanilla. Stir the wet mixture into the dry, mixing until well blended.

Press half the crust mixture into the prepared baking pan. With a spatula, gently spread the filling over the crust. Sprinkle the remaining crust mixture over the filling, making sure the dough gets into the corners of the pan. Gently pat the topping smooth. Bake until golden brown, 25–30 minutes. Cool completely before cutting into bars.

Cinnamon Spirals

These rich, buttery cookies melt in your mouth. Make them on a day when you have time to let the dough chill before rolling it out. If it is hard to slice the filled dough, refrigerate it again for an hour. This is a recipe that freezes well, so make an extra batch of dough to bake up another time.

DOUGH

2 cups whole-wheat pastry flour	3 tablespoons maple syrup
$1/2$ teaspoon sea salt	3–5 tablespoon ice water
10 tablespoons unsalted butter	

FILLING

$1/2$ cup pecans, or walnuts	Pinch sea salt
$1/2$ cup currants	1 teaspoon cinnamon
$1/2$ cup shredded unsweetened coconut	$1/2$ cup maple syrup

For dough: Sift the flour and salt into a bowl and make a well in the center. Cut the butter into small pieces and drop into the well. Using your fingertips, a pastry blender, or a fork, rub the butter into the flour to make a coarse, mealy texture. Add the maple syrup and quickly mix. Sprinkle the water over the mixture 1 tablespoon at a time, and, using a pastry blender or fork, incorporate just until the dough can be gathered into a ball. Flatten the dough into a thick rectangle or square, wrap in plastic wrap and refrigerate 30 minutes.

Preheat oven to 400 degrees. Oil a cookie sheet or line the pan with parchment paper.

For filling: Chop the nuts into fine pieces. In a bowl, combine the nuts with the currants, coconut, salt, cinnamon, and $1/4$ cup maple syrup.

Place the dough between 2 sheets of waxed paper on a marble slab or counter, and roll dough into a rectangle $3/8$ inch thick. Remove the top sheet of paper, and, using a pastry brush, spread the remaining maple syrup on the dough. Spread the nut mixture evenly over the dough. From one long end, roll up the dough and place seam side down on cutting board. With a sharp knife, cut the dough into 1-inch discs. Place discs on the prepared cookie sheet, leaving 1 inch between each spiral.

For a caramelized look and sweeter taste, brush the tops of the spirals with additional maple syrup.

Bake until golden brown, 10–20 minutes. Cool on the cookie sheet.

Sourdough Apple Bread Pudding

SERVES 6–8

It's hard waiting until dessert to enjoy this creamy, comforting pudding. Practically a meal in itself, it combines whole-grain bread with fruit, fiber, calcium, iron, and vitamin C. All we've left out are cream and sugar, showing how you can use soy beverage and maple syrup in their place. Consider making a double batch so you have leftovers for breakfast.

9–12 *slices sourdough bread*
  2 *cups plain or vanilla soy beverage*
  1 *large egg, or 1 tablespoon arrowroot*
  ³/₄ *cup maple syrup*
  2 *tablespoons vanilla extract*
3–4 *medium apples, peeled, cored, and sliced*

³/₄ *teaspoon cinnamon*
  Pinch nutmeg
  1 *teaspoon corn oil*
¹/₃ *cup raisins*

Remove crusts from the bread and tear into small pieces to make 6 cups. Place bread in a large bowl. Pour soy beverage over the bread pieces and set aside for an hour or longer. (You can let the bread soak, covered, in refrigerator overnight—the longer it sits, the more custardy the pudding.)

In a bowl, beat together the egg or arrowroot, ½ cup of the maple syrup, and the vanilla. Stir this into the bread mixture.

Toss the apples with the cinnamon and nutmeg. In a skillet, heat the corn oil and cook the apples with the remaining ¼ cup maple syrup and the raisins until mixture reduces considerably in volume. Allow the mixture to cool.

Preheat oven to 350 degrees. Oil a 9 × 9-inch baking pan or a 2-quart heat-proof casserole.

Pour the bread mixture into the baking pan and spread the apples on top. Alternatively, spoon dollops of apple onto the bread, then swirl the batter slightly with a spoon so that the apple mixture is randomly distributed throughout the pudding. Bake until a knife or cake tester inserted in the center comes out clean, 45–50 minutes. Serve warm or cold.

Chocolate Pudding

SERVES 2

Here's a version of this old-fashioned classic that everyone can enjoy, whether or not they use dairy products. Using both cocoa powder and chocolate gives it extra deep, chocolate flavor, which is enhanced by the taste of Sucanat.

2 tablespoons arrowroot
2 cups plain soy beverage
3 tablespoons Sucanat

2 tablespoons unsweetened cocoa powder
1 ounce unsweetened chocolate
1/2 teaspoon vanilla extract

In a small bowl, dissolve the arrowroot in 1/4 cup of the soy beverage.

In a saucepan, combine the remaining soy beverage with the Sucanat, cocoa powder, and chocolate. Cook over medium heat until the chocolate is melted. Reduce the heat and add the arrowroot mixture, stirring until the pudding thickens, about 6 minutes. Remove from heat and mix in the vanilla. Pour into individual serving bowls and refrigerate until cold.

Foolproof Whole-wheat Cake

This simple cake is dense with good nutrition, and it comes out right every time. It can be served as a simple cake or layered. We like it topped with Sweet Mirin Apricot Glaze (page 228) or layered, with Chocolate Maple Frosting (page 225) on top and in the middle.

1½ cups whole-wheat pastry flour
1½ cups unbleached white flour
¼ teaspoon sea salt
1 tablespoon nonaluminum baking powder

1 cup maple syrup
½ cup canola oil
2 eggs, beaten
1 teaspoon vanilla extract
1 cup plain soy beverage

Preheat oven to 350 degrees. Oil and flour a 9-inch round or square cake pan.

In a large bowl, sift together the flours, salt, and baking powder. In another bowl, beat together the maple syrup and oil. Stir the eggs, vanilla, and soy beverage into the maple syrup mixture. Stir the wet ingredients into the dry ingredients.

Pour batter into baking pan. Bake until a cake tester or toothpick inserted in the center comes out clean, 40–45 minutes.

Cool slightly on a rack before turning out to cool completely.

Chocolate Maple Frosting

Made with maple syrup in place of refined white sugar, this is a smooth, boiled frosting just like the 7-minute frosting Grandma used to make. Watching the egg whites turn into a creamy, soft meringue as you beat the hot syrup into them is a true example of culinary magic. Use this old-fashioned treat for icing and filling Foolproof Whole-wheat Cake (page 224), Wheat-free Chocolate Cake (page 226), or your own favorite layer cake or cupcakes.

½ cup maple syrup
3 egg whites

4 tablespoons cocoa powder
½ teaspoon vanilla

In small, heavy pan, bring the maple syrup to a boil. Cook until it reaches the soft ball stage on a candy thermometer, about 240 degrees. (If you don't have a candy thermometer, here's a simple, reliable way to test for soft ball. When the boiling syrup begins to thicken and becomes viscous, drop a small spoonful of the hot syrup into a glass half-filled with ice water. If the drop doesn't disintegrate but forms a soft ball that flattens a little of its own accord, the syrup is at the right temperature.)

While syrup is heating, in a large, clean, dry bowl, beat the eggwhites until they are very stiff. Very gradually, drizzle the boiling maple syrup in a fine stream into the egg whites while beating constantly with an electric beater on high speed. (Adding the hot syrup too quickly will cook the egg whites.) Fold in the cocoa powder and vanilla. Continue beating mixture at high speed until it is satin smooth, about 3 minutes.

Wheat-free Chocolate Cake

MAKES 2 (8-INCH) ROUND LAYERS

Although this recipe is dedicated to people with wheat allergies, who can't eat most cakes, it's hard keeping everyone else away from it. Teff has a sweet, earthy flavor that blends perfectly with chocolate. Its fine texture helps produce a light cake with a fine crumb. When you need a birthday cake, keep this recipe in mind.

CAKE

2¹/₂ cups teff flour

2 teaspoons nonaluminum baking powder

¹/₂ teaspoon baking soda

1 teaspoon cinnamon

¹/₂ teaspoon sea salt

1¹/₂ cups Sucanat, or maple granules

¹/₂ cup unsalted butter, softened

2 eggs, slightly beaten

1 cup plain soy beverage

1 teaspoon vanilla extract

2 ounces unsweetened chocolate, melted and cooled

ICING AND FILLING

³/₄ cup raspberry jam

1¹/₂ cups Chocolate Maple Frosting (page 225)

2 cups sliced almonds

Preheat oven to 350 degrees. Oil and flour two 8-inch round cake pans.

For cake: Into a large bowl, sift together the flour, baking powder, soda, cinnamon, and salt.

If the sugar is caked, put in a food processor or blender and process to a fine powder. In a large bowl, cream the sugar and butter together until fluffy. In another bowl, combine the eggs, soy beverage, vanilla, and chocolate. Stir into the creamed butter. Gently stir in the dry ingredients.

Divide the batter between the two prepared pans. Bake for 25 minutes, or until a toothpick or cake tester inserted in the center comes out clean. Cool on racks 5 minutes. Remove cakes from pans and cool completely on racks.

For icing: To ice the cake, place one cake layer on a plate and spread with raspberry jam. Position other layer, top side up, on the jam-covered layer. Spread entire cake with Chocolate Maple Frosting. Press almond slices into sides of cake.

VARIATION: For cupcakes, set paper baking cups in muffin tin, pour batter to ½ inch deep, and bake for 20 minutes or until a toothpick or cake tester inserted in the center comes out clean. Cool on racks. Frost with Chocolate Maple Frosting and decorate with sliced almonds or walnut halves. Makes 12 cupcakes.

Yogurt Gingerbread

MAKES 1 (11 × 7-INCH) CAKE

A liberal measure of ginger gives extra warmth to the flavor of this spicy gingerbread. Maple syrup rounds the edges of the assertive flavor of the molasses, while you get the benefit of the minerals in it. Serve with whipped cream, applesauce, or Tofu Sour Cream (page 163).

1 cup whole-wheat pastry flour	½ teaspoon ground nutmeg
1 cup unbleached white flour	½ cup canola oil
1 teaspoon baking soda	1½ cups maple syrup
1 teaspoon ground ginger	½ cup molasses
1 teaspoon cinnamon	2 eggs, separated
½ teaspoon ground cloves	½ cup plain yogurt

Preheat oven to 350 degrees. Oil and flour an 11 × 7-inch baking pan.

In a large bowl, sift together the flours, baking soda, ginger, cinnamon, cloves, and nutmeg. In another bowl, beat together the oil, maple syrup, and molasses. In a small bowl, lightly beat the egg yolks and add to the wet ingredients. Stir in the yogurt.

Combine the flour mixture with the wet ingredients, stirring well. In a large, very clean bowl, beat the egg whites until stiff, and fold them into the batter. Pour the batter into the prepared pan and bake 35–40 minutes, or until a toothpick or cake tester inserted into the center comes out clean.

Cool in the pan, on a rack.

Sweet Mirin Apricot Glaze

Brush this sweet glaze on loaf and bundt cakes and sweet buns, use it as a topping, or spread it between the layers of Foolproof Whole-wheat Cake (page 224). Thin with a bit more water and pour this glaze over baked apples, or stir it into applesauce. It tastes so good, you won't even think about the vitamins A and C and the beta carotene it adds.

5 *ounces apricot preserves*
1½ *tablespoons* mirin

1 *teaspoon lemon juice*
Pinch grated lemon or orange zest

In a small saucepan, combine the apricot fruit spread, *mirin,* lemon juice, and citrus zest with 2 tablespoons water and cook for about 5 minutes over low heat, stirring frequently. The glaze will first become thin, then thicken somewhat as it cooks. Allow to cool slightly before using, but don't cool completely or it will be too thick to spread.

Russian Apple Pie

Red wine, orange zest, and cherry fruit spread make this Russian-inspired apple pie decidedly different. The crisp whole-wheat crust goes perfectly with the moist and exuberant filling.

FILLING

8 large apples, cored and thinly sliced (about 4 pounds)
$^1/_2$ cup raisins
1 cup rice, or barley malt syrup
2 tablespoons red wine
1 tablespoon grated orange zest

$^1/_2$ teaspoon sea salt
$^1/_4$ cup whole-wheat pastry flour
$^1/_4$ cup almonds, toasted and chopped fine
2 tablespoons cherry jam, currant jelly, or raspberry preserves

CRUST

$1^1/_2$ cups whole-wheat flour
$1^1/_2$ cups whole-wheat pastry flour
$^3/_4$ cup apple juice

6 tablespoons corn oil
$^1/_2$ teaspoon sea salt

For filling: In a large pot, combine the apples, raisins, syrup, wine, orange zest, and salt. Cover, and cook over medium-low heat until apples are tender, 20–30 minutes. Stir occasionally so that fruit softens consistently. Mix in the flour, almonds, and jam, jelly, or preserves. Remove from heat. Cool about 15 minutes.

Preheat oven to 400 degrees. Oil a 10-inch pie pan.

For crust: In a large bowl, mix the flours together. Blend in the juice, oil, and salt, and knead briefly to form a smooth dough. Divide the dough into two equal portions and roll out to form two 12-inch circles. Lay one circle in the prepared pie pan. Fill with the apple mixture and cover with the remaining circle of rolled-out dough. Trim edges to leave $^3/_4$ inch of crust hanging over the edge. Crimp edges of top and bottom crust firmly together and poke holes in the top with a fork or slash decoratively with a sharp knife.

Bake until edges are golden brown, 12–15 minutes.

Ginger Crumb Pumpkin Pie

Here's a Thanksgiving favorite with an easy no-bake crust. Ginger snaps make a great match with the spicy filling and you can get them made without refined sugar at natural food stores. If you don't have time to cook fresh pumpkin, canned cooked pumpkin puree (*not* canned pumpkin pie filling) can be substituted. Purists may want to add a dash of nutmeg to the filling.

3 cups pumpkin chunks
$^1/_8$ teaspoon sea salt
$^1/_2$ cup honey, or brown rice syrup
2 tablespoons crushed kuzu *dissolved in*
  $^1/_2$ cup plain soy beverage

1 teaspoon cinnamon
$^1/_2$ teaspoon ground ginger
$^1/_8$ teaspoon ground cloves
1 teaspoon vanilla extract

CRUST

3 dozen $^1/_2$-inch ginger snap cookies
$1^1/_2$ tablespoons tahini mixed with $1^1/_2$
  tablespoons sesame oil

3 tablespoons honey, or brown rice syrup

For filling: Steam the pumpkin with the salt until tender, 30–45 minutes. Peel, discard the skin, and mash or puree the pumpkin. Place the pumpkin, honey, *kuzu* mixture, cinnamon, ginger, and cloves in a double boiler and cook over hot water, stirring occasionally, until thickened, 10–15 minutes. Stir in the vanilla and cool for 10 minutes.

For crust: Meanwhile, place ginger snaps in a blender or food processor and reduce to fine crumbs to yield $1^1/_2$ cups. Cut in the butter and tahini mixture, and turn mixture into a 9-inch pie pan. To form a crust, press mixture over bottom and up sides.

Pour pumpkin filling into pie shell. Serve chilled.

Pecan Sweet Potato Pie

Soul food can also be good for the body. If you want to avoid using butter, eggs, and refined sugar, this recipe proves that you can still make a luscious, creamy-textured version of this southern classic. Canned yams can be used in the filling, but take care not to burn them as they bake with the orange.

FILLING

2 oranges
4 medium sweet potatoes, peeled
1/2 teaspoon cinnamon
1/8 teaspoon nutmeg
2 teaspoons vanilla extract

2 pinches sea salt
1/2 cup maple syrup
3 tablespoons kuzu dissolved in
   3 tablespoons water

CRUST

3/4 cup whole-wheat pastry flour
3/4 cup unbleached white flour
   Pinch sea salt

1/4 cup canola oil
5 tablespoons ice water

TOPPING

1–1 1/2 cups pecan halves
2 tablespoons barley malt syrup

2 tablespoons maple syrup

Preheat oven to 350 degrees.

For filling: Cut zest from one of the oranges in strips. Grate the zest from the other orange. Squeeze the juice from both oranges.

In a baking dish, mix the strips of orange zest and half the orange juice with the whole sweet potatoes. Cover with foil and bake until the potatoes are done, about 1 hour. Discard the zest, and mash the potatoes with a fork (you should have approximately 4 cups of potatoes). If you prefer a smoother texture, whip the potatoes with a hand mixer. Add the remaining orange juice, the grated orange zest, and the cinnamon, nutmeg, vanilla, salt, maple syrup, and dissolved *kuzu*.

For crust: In a large bowl, combine the flours and salt. Pour on the oil and incorporate by rubbing quickly between your fingers; do not overmix. When the oil is distributed, sprinkle in the water 1 tablespoon at a time, stirring until the dough can be formed into a ball. Wrap the dough in waxed paper and chill 30 minutes. Remove from refrigerator a few minutes before using. Roll the dough into a circle 11 inches in diameter and place in a 9-inch pie plate, trimming the edges and crimping. Pour the sweet potato filling into the unbaked crust and even out the surface with a spatula.

For topping: Place the pecans on a cookie sheet and toast them until fragrant, about 10 minutes. Place pecans on top of the filling. Combine barley malt and maple syrup and sprinkle over nuts so they are shiny but not drenched. Bake the pie until the topping is bubbling and caramelized, and the crust is brown at the edges, about 40 minutes. Cool pie completely before slicing.

Boston Cream Pie

MAKES 1 (8-INCH) PIE

It's actually simple to make this old-fashioned treat. The recipe from which it was adapted required ¾ cup sugar, 6 egg yolks, white flour, and milk. If you are concerned about cutting back on these foods, here is an alternative way to make this classic.

LEMON PUDDING

1½ cups plain soy beverage or Almond
   Milk (page 241)
¼ cup maple syrup
⅛ teaspoon sea salt
1½ tablespoons agar flakes

1½ tablespoons kuzu *dissolved in*
   2 tablespoons cold water
1 teaspoon vanilla extract
1 tablespoon lemon juice
1 teaspoon grated lemon zest

CAKE

2 cups whole-wheat pastry flour
2 teaspoons nonaluminum baking
   powder
½ teaspoon baking soda
¼ teaspoon sea salt

⅓ cup corn or canola oil
1 cup brown rice syrup
1 teaspoon vanilla extract
1 egg, slightly beaten
¾ cup plain soy beverage, or water

CAROB ICING

3 tablespoons carob powder
1/3 cup boiling water
3 tablespoons maple syrup
1 tablespoon tahini

Pinch sea salt
2 teaspoons kuzu dissolved in
1 tablespoon cold water
1/4 teaspoon vanilla extract

For pudding: In a small saucepan over medium heat, combine the soy beverage or water, maple syrup, and salt. Sprinkle the agar flakes over mixture and bring to a simmer without stirring. Simmer 2 minutes, stirring occasionally. Stir the *kuzu* and add to the pudding while stirring briskly. Return to a simmer and cook 2 minutes. Remove from the heat and mix in the vanilla, lemon juice, and lemon zest. Chill pudding thoroughly. (The quickest method is to pour pudding into a bowl and place it, uncovered, in the freezer until firm.)

For cake: Preheat oven to 350 degrees. Oil two 8-inch round pans.

In a large bowl sift together the flour, baking powder, baking soda, and salt, and mix well. In a medium bowl, cream the oil with the maple syrup. Add the vanilla and beaten egg, and beat well. Mix in the soy beverage or water. Mix the dry ingredients into the wet. The batter should be thin enough to pour. If it is too thick, add a little more soy beverage or water.

Divide the batter between the prepared pans and bake 25–30 minutes, until the cakes pull away from the sides of the pan slightly and tops spring back when lightly pressed. Cool in the pan on wire racks for 10 minutes, then remove cakes from pans and cool thoroughly on the racks.

For icing: In a small saucepan, dissolve the carob powder in the boiling water. Add the maple syrup, tahini, and salt, and mix well. Mix the *kuzu* into the carob mixture. Bring to a simmer over medium heat while stirring briskly. Simmer 1–2 minutes, and remove from heat. Mix in the vanilla. Cool to lukewarm.

When cakes are cool, slice a small piece off the top of one layer so it will sit flat when inverted on a plate. Spread a 3/8-inch layer of the chilled pudding over the layer, leaving a 1/4-inch margin all around. Carefully place the top layer of cake on the pudding and cover the top (not sides) with carob icing.

Apple Berry Gel

The Japanese use agar, a sea vegetable, to make a refreshing gelled dessert called *kanten*. It has a firmer texture than gelatin and sets without refrigeration. You'll find agar in bars and flakes at natural food stores. Try it in place of pectin in jams, jellies, and molded desserts. Sometimes when we make this dessert, we puree the strawberries and mix them into the fruit juice before adding the agar.

4 cups apple or apple-strawberry juice
  Pinch sea salt
4 tablespoons agar flakes

2 tablespoons fresh lemon juice
2 cups fresh or frozen strawberries

In a saucepan, slowly bring the juice, salt, and agar to a simmer over medium heat without stirring. When the mixture begins to simmer, stir gently for 3 minutes. Remove from heat. Add the lemon juice. Place the strawberries in a deep bowl or mold and add the warm juice mixture. Set in a cool place or refrigerate until firm, 1–2 hours.

Ginger Peach Compote

Ripe peaches, fresh ginger, dried fruits, and sweet spices are combined to make this quick and tasty fruit dessert. Serve it topped with chopped nuts, granola, or vanilla yogurt. While it is sweet, this blend of fruits also makes an excellent side dish for grilled summer foods. You can use any 2-cup mixture of at least three different types of dried fruits when making this compote. It is a delightful way to take advantage of the concentrated iron, vitamin A, and minerals in dried fruits.

$^1\!/_2$ cup dried figs
$^1\!/_2$ cup dried apricots
$^1\!/_2$ cup dried pitted prunes
$^1\!/_2$ cup raisins
$^1\!/_4$ teaspoon allspice
$^1\!/_4$ teaspoon cinnamon
$^1\!/_8$ teaspoon ground cloves
1 teaspoon ground ginger

$^1\!/_2$ teaspoon ground cardamom
2 cups peeled and diced ripe peaches
   (about 1 pound)
Pinch sea salt
1 teaspoon grated orange zest
$^1\!/_2$ cup orange juice
1 teaspoon Ginger Juice (page 241)

Remove the hard tips of the fig stems, and chop the figs into $^1\!/_2$-inch pieces. Chop the dried apricots and prunes into $^1\!/_2$-inch pieces. Rinse all the dried fruit in a strainer to remove any dust. Place dried fruit in a large saucepan with 1 cup of water. Cover and bring to a boil. Lower the heat and simmer until the fruit has plumped up, about 10 minutes. Add the allspice, cinnamon, cloves, ginger, and cardamom to the simmering fruit. Add the peaches, salt, orange zest, and orange juice to the fruit and stir. Lower heat to simmer gently for about 10 minutes.

Stir the ginger juice into the fruit and continue to cook 2–3 minutes. Remove from heat and allow to cool. Stir and serve compote warm or at room temperature.

To store, refrigerate, covered, in a nonreactive container with a tight-fitting cover.

Peach Glacé

This is a refreshing, no-fuss, no-fat dessert. If you wish, you can pour the peach mixture into plastic freezer molds to make "peach pops" for the kids—or the kid in you. Peaches are a good source of vitamins A and C.

3 cups peeled and diced fresh peaches
   (about 1¹/₂ pounds)
¹/₂ cup peach fruit spread
1 tablespoon fresh lemon juice

1 teaspoon vanilla extract
Pinch sea salt
Fresh mint leaves or frozen green
   grapes, for garnish

Combine the peaches, jam, lemon juice, vanilla, and salt in a food processor and puree until smooth. Sample for sweetness. Add additional preserves or honey to taste, if desired. Pour the fruit mixture into a shallow, freezer-proof container.

Freeze 2–4 hours. The peach mixture should be firm but not rock-solid. Serve when a scoop will hold its shape in a dessert bowl. Garnish with mint leaves or frozen green grapes.

To make a lighter dessert, you can place the lightly frozen peach mixture into the food processor for a second time, to add extra air, then return mixture to the freezer for 10–20 minutes before serving.

If the dessert freezes too solid to serve, allow it to thaw enough to spoon into a food processor. Blend 30–60 seconds. Return to the freezer for about 20 minutes. This will make it evenly soft throughout. Serve by scraping across the top with an ice cream spoon or large serving spoon to get an ice-cream parlor curl.

Raspberry Dessert Sauce

This sauce makes any dessert special. Serve over cake, pancakes, waffles, frozen yogurt, or nondairy frozen desserts. Raspberries are excellent sources of vitamin C, fiber, and potassium. They also contain ellagic acid, a natural substance that studies suggest may help prevent certain types of cancer.

1 cup frozen raspberries, without sugar
1/2 cup juice from thawed berries
Grated zest of 1 lemon
1/4 cup fresh lemon juice

1/4 cup maple syrup
2 teaspoons arrowroot dissolved in
1 tablespoon cold water

In a bowl, thaw the raspberries. In a small saucepan over medium heat, combine the raspberries and their juice, the lemon zest, lemon juice, and maple syrup. Cook until the mixture begins to boil. Whisk the arrowroot mixture into the hot sauce. Stir until smooth, and remove from heat. Serve sauce chilled.

13. The Natural Health Pantry

BASIC RECIPES

A few recipes in this book call for an ingredient which has to be made up, using its own simple recipe. We've put these recipes here to make it easier for you. These are recipes you can also use to perk up dishes you already know.

Garam Masala

Masala means a mixture of spices; *garam* means hot. A *masala* differs from curry powder in two basic ways: the spices in a *masala* are roasted first, then ground, and a *masala* is added at the end of preparation, not at the beginning, as with curry powder. There are many variations of this classic recipe, and this one is a hot version from southern India. Try sprinkling some *garam masala* over plain rice or on baked acorn squash and other vegetables before serving.

20 *cardamom pods*
1 *stick cinnamon*
1 *tablespoon whole cloves*
2 *tablespoons black peppercorns*
3 *tablespoons cumin seeds*

3 *tablespoons black mustard seeds*
3 *tablespoons coriander seeds*
3 *tablespoons fenugreek seeds*
3 *tablespoons grated unsweetened coconut*

Preheat oven to 350 degrees. Break open the cardamom pods, remove seeds, and discard pods. Break cinnamon stick into small pieces using a kitchen mallet or rolling pin. Spread all ingredients except coconut on a baking sheet and roast 10 minutes, shaking the pan several times during roasting, until the spices are fragrant.

Add the coconut and roast 5 minutes more, or until the coconut turns golden. Remove from oven, cool, and grind to medium-fine in a blender or electric spice mill. (A food processor will not create a fine enough grind.)

Garam masala will keep for up to 3 months stored in a cool, dark place in an airtight container.

Almond Milk

The delicate flavor of this milk goes nicely in cream soups such as **Mushroom Almond Bisque (page 31)**. It also makes a pleasant sauce served with fresh strawberries or over **Ginger Peach Compote (page 235)**.

¹/₃ cup blanched almonds (see Note)

Place the almonds in a blender with 1 cup water and process until smooth.

NOTE: Blanched almonds are sold at the supermarket and some natural food stores. To make them yourself, boil a pot of water. Drop the almonds into the boiling water, remove pot from heat, and let sit 1 minute. Drain and rub to remove the skins from the hot almonds. Refrigerated it keeps for 2–3 days.

Ginger Juice

Squeezing the juice from fresh ginger extracts its concentrated flavor. In some recipes, this "essence" of ginger is preferable to the fiber and small pieces of minced ginger. It's the perfect way to add ginger flavor to both uncooked and cooked dishes, including sauces, salad dressings, and fruit salads. Ginger juice is also useful for flavoring some desserts, such as pie fillings and bread puddings, where you might enjoy the flavor of fresh ginger more than that of ground. If possible, use a ginger grater, which has tiny teeth designed to turn even the most fibrous ginger into a creamy puree. This inexpensive tool is sold at Asian and natural food stores, as well as at stores that sell cooking equipment.

Grate the fresh ginger very fine. In a piece of cheesecloth or clean cotton towel, squeeze the grated ginger to get the amount of juice needed. Add the ginger juice to the ingredients in your recipe and mix to blend.

Unsweetened Coconut Milk

MAKES 4 CUPS

Most commercially produced coconut products contain sulfites to help keep them white. The shredded coconut sold in supermarkets is sweetened, as well. Using fresh coconut is a way to avoid these problems, though it can be a time-consuming process. Unsweetened grated coconut is sold in most natural food stores. If you want to keep some on hand, store it in a tightly sealed container in the freezer. When a recipe calls for coconut milk, here is the simplest, fastest way to obtain it.

5 cups dried, unsweetened coconut

In a large pot, boil 5 cups of water and add the coconut. Remove pot from heat and let stand 20 minutes. In a blender or food processor, puree the coconut and its liquid 1 cup at a time, 3 minutes per batch, until the coconut is finely pureed. Pour the blended material into several layers of cheesecloth resting in a strainer over a bowl. Let the coconut milk drain through the strainer.

After most of the milk has drained, pick up the cloth with the coconut in it and squeeze hard to get the rest of the coconut milk. Refrigerated, the milk will keep 4 or 5 days.

NOTE: You can repeat this procedure, reusing the coconut and 3 cups water, to make a thin coconut milk that has a less intense flavor. It is also lower in fat.

Savory Bread Crumbs

This basic recipe works well with a variety of spice combinations. You can use oregano or thyme instead of basil.

½ cup bread crumbs
3–4 tablespoons extra virgin olive oil
¼ teaspoon sea salt
1 clove garlic, minced fine

1 pinch cayenne pepper
2 tablespoons finely minced parsley
1 tablespoon finely minced fresh basil

Mix all ingredients together. Use as a stuffing or on top of vegetables.

GLOSSARY OF INGREDIENTS

As you read through recipes in this book, many ingredients may be unfamiliar to you. In the chapter introductions, we talk about foods the recipes in that chapter focus on. Still, there are items you may not recognize. This glossary explains what they are, tells why they are useful foods to include in a whole-food diet, and suggests where to buy them.

Agar (also Agar-Agar and Kanten)—A colorless, tasteless sea vegetable used to gel liquids. It makes a firm gel which sets at room temperature, without chilling. Agar is found in flakes and bar form at natural food stores. The flakes are easier to use.

Amasake (or Amazake)—A sweet beverage rich in complex carbohydrates, it is made by introducing *koji* (a live bacterial culture) into cooked sweet glutinous rice, causing fermentation. Used mainly as a refreshing drink, *amasake* can also be thickened to make puddings, and used as an ingredient in baking. Look for it, plain and in flavors, in bottles in the refrigerated section and in aseptic boxes on the shelves at natural food stores.

Arrowroot—A white powder used for thickening sauces that is made from a tuber of the same name. Arrowroot becomes clear when cooked. To avoid clumping, always dissolve in cold water before adding to a hot liquid. It is available in the spice section at supermarkets and at natural food stores.

Barley Malt Syrup—Sweeter than Brown Rice Syrup but with about half the sweetness of sugar, this thick, dark sweetener is made from sprouted, roasted barley. It has a rich, roasted flavor somewhere between that of molasses and honey. Useful for both baking and cooking, do not confuse the syrup with barley malt powder, which is much sweeter. Measure this sticky sweetener with an oiled spoon or cup.

Brewer's Yeast (also Nutritional Yeast)—Nonleavening yeast used in making beer. This yeast is used in vegetarian cooking because it is a rich source of B vitamins and has a full flavor. It is sold as a powder in natural food stores.

Brown Rice Syrup—A thick, honeylike natural sweetener made from cooked brown rice and sprouted barley or barley enzymes. Often used in baking, this amber sweetener has a particularly mild flavor. To measure it, use an oiled spoon or cup.

Brown Rice Vinegar—A mild, amber vinegar made with brown rice. Look for brands made from organically grown rice. Rice vinegar is expensive because it takes more than 12 months to prepare. It is brewed in two ways; either made from sake (Japanese rice wine), water, and bacteria known as "mother of vinegar," or from cooked rice, *koji* (a bacterial culture), water, and a vinegar "mother." It can be found in natural food stores.

Burdock—A brown-skinned root, up to 3 feet long, that looks like a thin, hairy parsnip. Peeled and cut in matchsticks, slices, or chips, it adds an earthy flavor to winter soups and stews. Called *gobo* in Japan, burdock is believed to have fortifying, tonic properties. Fresh burdock, sold in natural and Japanese food stores, keeps 3 to 4 days, refrigerated and wrapped in plastic wrap. Wild burdock is common throughout the United States and is often found growing as a weed.

Chinese Five-Spice Powder—A pungent mixture of ground cinnamon, cloves, fennel seeds, star anise, and Szechuan peppercorns. It is used for seasoning in Asian cooking. It can be found at Asian food stores and in the ethnic food section of some supermarkets.

Dashi—A smoky-flavored broth used in Japanese cooking for soup stock, it is traditionally the base for miso soup. Most often, it is made using shaved bonito flakes. Vegetarian versions of *dashi* can be made using *kombu,* a dried sea vegetable, or mushrooms.

Garam Masala—A blend of dry-roasted ground spices used in Indian cooking. The combination of "warm" spices can vary and some recipes use up to twelve kinds, including black pepper, cinnamon, cloves, coriander, cumin, fennel, mace, and nutmeg. This seasoning is usually added toward the end of cooking or sprinkled on dishes just before serving. It can easily be made at home, or it can be found at Indian food stores and in the gourmet section of some supermarkets. (See also page 240.)

Kombu—A dried sea vegetable sold in wide dark green strips, sometimes with a powdery, white coating. This member of the kelp family contains glutamic acid, which serves as a flavor enchancer for soups, stews, and other cooked foods. It also may help reduce flatulence when cooked with dried beans. Do not rinse before using; any powder on the surface is part of the flavor element in this sea vegetable. It is sold in packages and in bulk at natural food sores.

Kuzu—A tasteless starch used for thickening sauces and desserts, including puddings, *kuzu* comes as white, pebblelike lumps made from the roots of the kudzu vine. It may be used in place of arrowroot or cornstarch, and like them, it should be dissolved in cold water before being added to a hot liquid to avoid clumping. Foods made using *kuzu* may have soothing properties for the digestion. It is found in small packets and in bulk in natural food stores.

Mirin—A sweet Japanese rice wine used in cooking. This syrupy, low-alcohol wine is made from sweet glutinous rice fermented with water and *koji* (a grain-based culture). It adds flavor to sauces and other dishes. Check the label to be sure no corn syrup or sugar has been

added. It is available in Asian and natural food stores.

Miso—A salty, rich-flavored fermented paste used in Japanese and Chinese cooking. It is made from soybeans inoculated with *koji* (a culture of *Aspergillus oryzae* bacteria), and salt, and aged from 2 months up to 3 years. There are many kinds of miso. They may include other grains, such as rice or barley. There is also a chick-pea miso. Misos range in color from dark brown, or red, to pale beige or white. Darker misos contain more salt and protein than the mellow and sweet varieties. The unpasteurized, naturally aged, fresh miso sold in the refrigerated section at natural food stores contains live bacteria: naturally aged pasteurized miso sold at Asian food stores does not. In cooking, miso is often used as a flavor enhancer. It may be added to a dish early on, or mixed in toward the end. Once miso is added, avoid boiling: intense heat destroys enzymes in the miso.

Natural Soy Sauce—These are soy sauces naturally fermented for a year or more, using soybeans, salt, water, and, possibly, wheat. Commercially made soy sauces are made in a week or less, using hydrolyzed vegetable protein, caramel coloring, and corn syrup. *Shoyu* is both the generic Japanese word for soy sauce and the name for those that contain wheat. *Tamari*, sometimes used to mean soy sauce, can also mean a kind made without wheat. Because these terms are used in more than one way, it's best to check the label when buying soy sauce, particularly if you must avoid wheat.

Nigari—The coagulating agent traditionally used in making tofu. Made by evaporating seawater, it is primarily composed of magnesium chloride and trace minerals.

Nonaluminum baking powder—A leavening agent used in baking. Most commercial brands of double-acting baking powder contain sodium aluminum sulfate, which may be harmful to your health. Natural food stores carry brands, particularly Rumford and Featherlight, that do not contain aluminum salts.

Sea Salt—Made by the costly process of evaporating seawater, which leaves in valuable trace minerals lost when salt is refined into table salt. Table salt contains additives, including chemicals to make it free-flowing, potassium iodide, dextrose, and sodium bicarbonate. Sea salt is found at natural food stores and supermarkets in fine grain and coarse crystals.

Seitan—A high-protein food made from the gluten in wheat flour. Good in stews and soups, it can be made from scratch, or bought already prepared. Natural food stores carry Vital Wheat, a high-gluten flour used for making seitan, as well as chunks of meaty-looking, ready-to-use seitan, packaged in richly flavored broth. It is found refrigerated in tubs and on the shelf in jars. Seitan is also used to make meatlike products, including vegetarian sausage and cold cuts.

Sesame Oil—Recipes in this book call for two kinds of sesame oil. Golden sesame oil has a mild, nutty flavor. Use it on salads and in cooking. Look for less refined brands that are cold, expeller-pressed, at supermarkets and natural food stores. Intensely flavored, aromatic, dark sesame oil, also known as roasted or oriental sesame oil, is best used for flavoring. It burns easily at high temperatures so add it to cooked dishes at the end, as a finishing oil. Dark sesame oil can also be found at supermarkets, Asian and natural food stores.

Soy Beverage (Soy Milk)—A beige liquid made from soybeans and water. Some brands also contain an unrefined sweetener, such as barley malt. Soy beverage is sold in plain and flavored forms, as well as in low-fat and calcium-fortified versions. The taste varies greatly from brand to brand; experiment to find one you prefer. Often used in cooking to replace cow's milk, soy beverages turn dark or grayish when heated. They can be found in supermarkets by the coffee section and in natural food stores.

Soy Cheese—Made using soy milk in place of cow's milk, soy cheese comes in many forms, from soft mozzarella to Cheddar and grated Parmesan. Like dairy cheese, soy cheeses can be sliced, shredded, and melted.

Sucanat—A granulated, unrefined natural sweetener made of evaporated, organic sugarcane juice. It retains the trace minerals removed from refined sugar. Its definite flavor can be pronounced in some dishes. Found in natural food stores.

Tahini (Sesame Paste)—A rich, peanut-buttery paste used in Middle Eastern and Asian cooking. For whole-food cooking, look for tahini made from unhulled, toasted sesame seeds rather than the Middle Eastern kind, usually found in cans, made from hulled, untoasted seeds. It can be found in supermarkets and natural foods stores.

Tamarind—A tart-tasting Asian fruit used in Asian and Middle Eastern cooking. Dried tamarind, tamarind paste, and tamarind syrup can be found in Indian food stores. The sweetened tamarind syrup sold in Italian and Hispanic food stores is used for making cold drinks; it is not suitable for cooking.

Teff—A tiny, celery-seed-sized grain rich in protein. This gluten-free grain is easily ground into flour in a blender. Comes in red, white, and brown varieties that vary slightly in flavor but may be used interchangeably for making pancakes and baked goods. It can be found in natural food stores.

Tempeh—A high-protein soy food, it is made by fermenting crushed, cooked soy beans which have been inoculated with the bacteria *Rhizopus oligosporous*. A staple food of Indonesia, tempeh is good in stews, or marinated and fried or grilled. Its distinctive, yeasty flavor makes a slab of tempeh a good stand-in for a hamburger. Other grains, such as brown rice, millet, or quinoa, are often combined with soy beans when making tempeh; these versions have a milder flavor.

Udon—A kind of plump, white Japanese noodle, made from wheat flour. These thick, chewy noodles are good in soup or topped with a sauce. They can also be eaten cold in salads. Natural food stores carry *udon* made from brown rice as well as from whole-wheat flour.

Umeboshi—A small Japanese plum, salted, pickled, and aged using red shiso leaf for flavoring and as a natural preservative. It also gives the pickled plums their rosy color. Umeboshi are used, either whole or in a paste, as a condiment and an aid to digestion. *Umeboshi* vinegar contains the rose-pink liquid that rises from the surface of *umeboshi* plums. It has a unique, salty and puckery flavor, with a tang of citrus. All forms of *umeboshi* are found in Japanese and natural food stores. If not buying *umeboshi* in a natural food store, check to be sure no artificial coloring is used.

Wakame—A mild-flavored, crunchy sea vegetable used mainly in salads. It is harvested along the coasts of Japan, China, and Korea. A similar sea vegetable, *alaria,* is collected in the waters off Maine and the Pacific Northwest. They can be used interchangeably. *Wakame* is sold at both Japanese and natural food stores.

Wasabi—A gnarled, brown root related to horseradish, it grows in Japanese mountain streams. Dried and ground to a powder, then combined with water to make a bright, pale-green paste, *wasabi* is mostly used as a condiment, especially on sushi and with sashimi. It can be found in Japanese and Asian food stores and natural food stores either in powdered form, in cans, or in tubes as a paste. Like mustard, *wasabi* looses heat and flavor over time; it is best mixed or portioned out just before using.

MAIL ORDER

If local supermarkets, ethnic, or natural food stores do not carry items you need, here is a list of resources you can get them from. Many offer products that are certified organic. (Ask when you contact them whether the certification they offer is third party or based on some other form of verification) Many of them can send you a catalogue on request.

GENERAL:

Natural Ark Trading Company
120 South East Avenue
Fayetteville, AR 72701

Neshaminy Valley Natural Foods
    Distributor, Ltd.
5 Louise Drive
Ivyland, PA 18974
215-443-5545
Minimum order $100.

Walnut Acres
Penns Creek, PA 17862
800-433-3993

SPECIALTY:

BEANS

Bean Bag
818 Jefferson Street
Oakland, CA 94607
800-845-BEAN

Dean & DeLuca Retail and Mail-Order
    Department
560 Broadway
New York, NY 10012
800-221-7714

Breads (Whole-Grain)

Berkshire Mountain Bakery
P.O. Box 785
Housatonic, MA 01236
800-274-3412

French Meadow Bakery
2601 Lyndale Avenue South
Minneapolis, MN 55972
612-870-4740

Chili Peppers

Los Chileros de Neuvo Mexico
P.O. Box 6215
Santa Fe, NM 87501
505-471-6967

Chinese

The Oriental Pantry
423 Great Road
Acton, MA 01720
800-823-0368

Citrus Fruits

Earl Ebersol Farms
27828 S.W. 127th Avenue
Homestead, FL 33032
305-247-3905

Dried Fruit

Chukar Cherry Company
320 Wine Country Road
P.O. Box 510
Prosser, WA 99350
800-624-9544

Timber Crest Farms
4791 Dry Creek Road
Healdsberg, CA 95448
707-433-8251

Garlic

Haypoint Farm
Box 292
Sugar Island
Sault Sainte Marie, MI 49783
906-632-1280

Greens and Vegetables

Diamond Organics
Freedom, CA 95019
800-922-2396

Herbs and Spices

Fox Hill Farm
444 West Michigan Avenue, Box 79
Parma, MI 49269
517-531-3179
Ships fresh herbs.

Frontier Cooperative Herbs
Box 299
Norway, IA 52318
800-669-3275

Meadowbrook Herb Garden
R.R. Box 138
Wyoming, RI 02898
401-539-7603

International Condiments/Vinegars, etc.

G. B. Ratto
821 Washington Street
Oakland, CA 94607
800-325-3483

Jams and Preserves

American Spoon Foods
411 East Lake Street
Petosky, MI 47770
800-222-5886
Offers no-sugar-added Spoon Fruits
and dried fruits.

Kozlowski Farms
5566 Gravenstein Highway
Forestville, CA 95436
707-887-1857
Offers no-sugar-added conserves,
butters, and chutneys.

Wood's Cider Mill
R.F.D. 2, Box 477
Springfield, VT 05156
802-263-5547
Offers cider jelly, cider syrup, boiled
cider, and maple syrup.

Maple Syrup

Uncle Joel's Pure Maple Syrup
Route 1
Hammond, WI 54105
715-796-5395

Nuts

Blue Heron Farm
P.O. Box 68
Runsey, CA 95679
916-796-3799

Onions

Bland Farms
P.O. Box 506
Glennville, GA 30427
800-VIDALIA

Walla Walla Gardener's Association
210 North Eleventh Street
Walla Walla, WA 99362
800-552-5014

Porridge, Cereal, and Breakfast Foods

Arrowhead Mills
110 South Lawton
Hereford, TX 79405
806-364-0730
Sells mainly through stores, but will
ship to people who do not live near a
retail outlet.

Fiddler's Green Farm
RFD 1
Box 656
Belfast, ME 04915

Quinoa

Quinoa Company
2300 Central Avenue, Suite G
Boulder, CO 80301
800-237-2304
Offers quinoa grain and pastas.
Minimum order twelve boxes.

Rices

Lundberg Family Farms
P.O. Box 369
Richvale, CA 95947
916-822-4551

Sea Vegetables

Maine Seaweed Company
P.O. Box 57
Steuben, ME 04680
207-546-2875

Mendocino Sea Vegetable Company
P.O. Box 372
Navarro, CA 95463

Wheat-Free/Gluten-Free

Allergy Resource
195 Huntington Beach Drive
Colorado Springs, CO 80921
719-488-3630

En-R-G Foods, Inc.
P.O. Box 84487
Seattle, WA 98124
800-331-5222

Wild Rice

Black Duck Company
9640 Vincent Avenue South
Bloomington, MN 55431
612-884-3471

Northern Lakes Wild Rice Co.
P.O. Box 28
Cass Lake, MN 56633
218-355-6369

Bibliography

Baird, Pat. *The Pyramid Cookbook*. New York: Henry Holt, 1993.

Goldbeck, Nikki, and David Goldbeck. *American Wholefoods Cuisine*. New York: New American Library, 1983.

Greene, Bert. *The Grains Cookbook*. New York: Workman, 1988.

Hausman, Patricia, and Judith Benn Hurley. *The Healing Foods*. Emmaus, Pa.: Rodale Press, 1989.

Kilham, Christopher. *The Bread & Circus Whole Food Bible*. Reading, Mass.: Addison Wesley, 1991.

Pickarski, Brother Ron. *Friendly Foods*. Berkeley: Ten Speed Press, 1991.

Rinzler, Carol Ann. *The Complete Book of Food*. New York: World Almanac, 1987.

Sass, Lorna. *Recipes from an Ecological Kitchen*. New York: William Morrow, 1992.

Shurtleff, William, and Akiko Aoyagi. *The Book of Miso*. New York: Ballantine Books, 1976.

For Mail Order Information:

Devi, Yamuna. *Yamuna's Table*. New York: Dutton, 1992.

Lazar, Elysa, and Eve Miceli. *Elysa Lazar's Shop by Mail*. New York: Lazar Media Group, 1992.

Marlin, John Tepper. *The Catalogue of Healthy Food*. New York: Bantam, 1990.

Wiegand, Lee. *The Food Catalogue*. New York: Clarkson N. Potter, 1990.

Liquid and Dry Measure Equivalencies

CUSTOMARY	METRIC
¼ teaspoon	1.25 milliliters
½ teaspoon	2.5 milliliters
1 teaspoon	5 milliliters
1 tablespoon	15 milliliters
1 fluid ounce	30 milliliters
¼ cup	60 milliliters
⅓ cup	80 milliliters
½ cup	120 milliliters
1 cup	240 milliliters
1 pint (2 cups)	480 milliliters
1 quart (4 cups; 32 ounces)	960 milliliters (.96 liter)
1 gallon (4 quarts)	3.84 liters
1 ounce (by weight)	28 grams
¼ pound (4 ounces)	114 grams
1 pound (16 ounces)	454 grams
2.2 pounds	1 kilogram (1,000 grams)

Oven Temperature Equivalents

DESCRIPTION	FAHRENHEIT	CELSIUS
Cool	200	90
Very slow	250	120
Slow	300–325	150–160
Moderately slow	325–350	160–180
Moderate	350–375	180–190
Moderately hot	375–400	190–200
Hot	400–450	200–230
Very hot	450–500	230–260

Index

Italian dishes:
    baked polenta squares, 50
    grilled fish with salsa verde, 136–37
    maple almond biscotti, 216–17
    minestrone americano, 27
    parsley pepper poaching sauce, 172
    roasted peppers with anchovies, 95
    tomato olivada crostini, 207
    see also pasta
ital run down, 104

jalapeño onion chutney, 174
Jamaican dishes:
    baked fish fillets, 132
    ital run down, 104
jambalaya, quinoa, 48
jams, mail-order sources for, 250
Japanese dishes:
    amasake dressing, 153
    fish soup, 28
    fried noodles, 56
    shiitake and watercress soup, 24
Jerusalem artichoke pasta, 54
juices, 178, 212
    ginger, 241

kabuli chole, 115
kale, 88, 89
    salad, Cajun, 106–7
kamut, 38, 54
kanten, 234, 243
kasha, 37
    and onion piroshki, 52
    tabouli, 51
kidney beans, 113
kiwi, 212
    orange, and watercress salad, 145
kombu, 23, 112, 245
kuzu, 245

leeks:
    baked sole with shiitake mushrooms and,
        135–36
    vinaigrette, 90
legumes, *see* bean(s)

lemon:
    and blood orange salad, 144
    cinnamon beets, 93
    escarole soup, 25
    pudding, 232–33
    sesame cookies, 218
lentil(s), 112, 113
    Himalayan, 117
    red, curried pâté, 198–99
    red, soup, Indian spiced, 32
lima beans, 112, 113, 114
linguini:
    aglio e olio, 57
    with dark greens and beans, 59
Louisiana cooking:
    quinoa jambalaya, 48
    red beans and rice, 121
    shrimp stew, 139
lysine, 36, 37, 70

macaroni and green bean salad, 64
mackerel, 127
    fillets, Jamaican baked, 132
magnesium, 35
mahi-mahi, 127
mail-order sources, 248–51
main courses, *see* entrées
mangoes, 212
maple (syrup), 214
    almond biscotti, 216–17
    chocolate frosting, 225
    mail-order source for, 250
maque choux, 94
mayonnaise, dilled soy, 149
Mediterranean dishes:
    bean salad, 124
    salad with balsamic vinaigrette, 152–53
    see also Italian dishes; pasta
methionine, 70
Mexican dishes:
    bean spread, 123
    sweet pepper pinto bean chili, 120
millet, 37–38
    and rice with spicy peanut sauce, 41–42
minestrone americano, 27